WITHDRAWN

Water Worlds
The Antarctic

Cheryl Hook

for the Australian Museum

This edition first published in 2002 in the United States of America by Chelsea House Publishers, a subsidiary of Haights Cross Communications

All rights reserved. No part of this publication may be reproduced or transmitted in any form or by any means without the written permission of the publisher.

Chelsea House Publishers
1974 Sproul Road, Suite 400
Broomall, PA 19008–0914

The Chelsea House world wide web address is www.chelseahouse.com

Library of Congress Cataloging-in-Publication Data Applied for.
ISBN 0-7910-6566-9

First published in 2000 by
Macmillan Education Australia Pty Ltd
627 Chapel Street, South Yarra, Australia, 3141

Copyright © Australian Museum 2000

Australian Museum Series Editor: Carolyn MacLulich
Australian Museum Scientific Adviser: Doug Hoese
Australian Museum Publishing Unit: Jenny Saunders and Kate Lowe

Edited by Anne McKenna
Typeset in Bembo
Printed in Hong Kong
Text and cover design by Leigh Ashforth @ watershed art & design
Illustrations by Peter Mather

Acknowledgements

For Lauren and Robert, who will one day go exploring

The author and publishers are grateful to the following for permission to use copyright material:

Front cover:
        Main photo: Kathie Atkinson
        Inset photo: Jean-Paul Ferrero/AUSCAPE
Back cover: Jean-Paul Ferrero/AUSCAPE

Colin Monteath/AUSCAPE, pp. 15, 20 (bottom), 21; D. Parer & E. Parer-Cook/AUSCAPE, pp. 10, 27 (bottom); Doug Allan-Oxford Scientific Films/AUSCAPE, p. 17 (top); Dr Nick Gales/Lochman Transparencies, p. 18; Graham Robertson/AUSCAPE, pp. 13, 27 (top), 30; J. Bennett-Peter Arnold/AUSCAPE, p. 11 (bottom); Jean-Paul Ferrero/AUSCAPE, pp. 3, 11 (top), 12, 16, 17 (bottom), 19, 20 (top), 23 (top and bottom); Kathie Atkinson, pp. 14, 22; Kevin Deacon/Ocean Earth Images, p. 9; Michael Whitehead/AUSCAPE, p. 29; Robyn Stewart/AUSCAPE, pp. 4-5; Tui De Roy/AUSCAPE, p. 25.

While every care has been taken to trace and acknowledge copyright, the publishers tender their apologies for any accidental infringements where copyright has proved untraceable.

Contents

What is the Antarctic?

The Antarctic is a huge area of land and ocean that covers the southern end of the Earth. The South Pole is at the center of the Antarctic.

The large land area is called Antarctica. Antarctica is the fifth biggest **continent** and covers 14.25 million square kilometers (5.5 million square miles). It is one and a half times the size of the United States of America. It is the highest, driest and coldest of all the continents. Antarctica's environment and climate are ruled by wind, ice and snow. Very few plants and animals, including humans, live there all year round.

The huge, cold Southern Ocean surrounds Antarctica. In winter, part of the ocean closest to Antarctica freezes over, creating large areas of sea ice. Many different types of animals live on the **sea ice** and in the Southern Ocean where they get their food.

Subantarctic islands, such as South Georgia and Macquarie Island, are dotted throughout the Southern Ocean. These islands have slightly warmer climates than Antarctica. Because they are warmer, more plants and animals, including humans, live on and visit the subantarctic islands.

≋ **Icebergs** float in the ocean. In the background is part of Antarctica called the Antarctic Peninsula.

Where is the Antarctic?

Antarctic Circle: an imaginary line around Antarctica, drawn on the globe at 66 degrees South. This marks the boundary of Antarctica.

Antarctic Convergence: the point where warm water from the north mixes with cold water from the south. This marks the boundary of the Antarctic.

Antarctica: a large area of land covered with ice and snow.

South Pole: the place marking the most southerly point on the Earth.

Transantarctic Mountains: these mountains are mostly covered with snow and ice and are more than 4,000 meters (13,124 feet) high.

Mount Erebus: an active volcano 3,794 meters (12,450 feet) high.

McMurdo: a place where scientists live and study in Antarctica.

Vostok: a Russian weather station in Eastern Antarctica.

Beardmore Glacier: a **glacier** that cuts through the Transantarctic Mountains to the Ross **Ice Shelf**.

Lambert Glacier: the largest glacier on Antarctica.

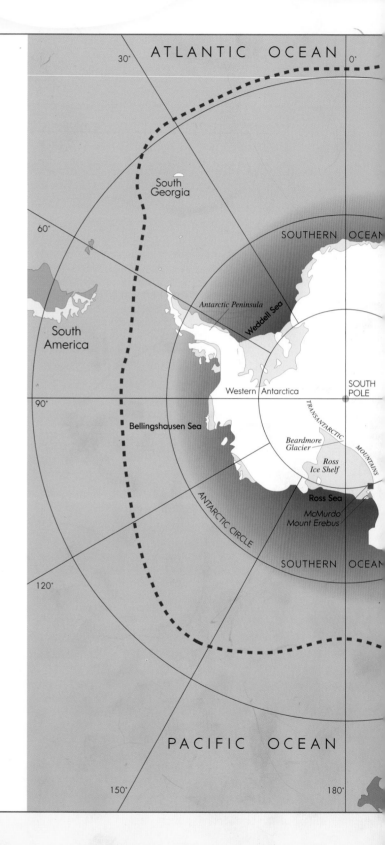

The map below shows the area covered by the Antarctic. Important places and features of the Antarctic are labelled.

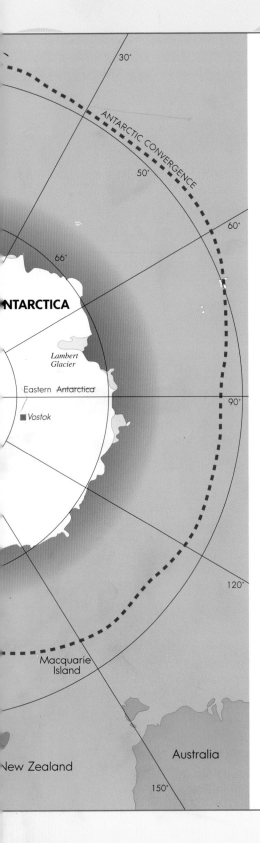

Antarctic Peninsula: a finger-shaped piece of land that sticks out into the Southern Ocean.

Eastern Antarctica: a place that has very old low-lying land. This land is covered by a thick sheet of ice called an ice cap that is shaped like a dome and is more than 4,000 meters (13,124 feet) thick in some places.

Western Antarctica: a place with many mountains and valleys that are covered by three dome-shaped sheets of ice called ice caps. Each ice cap is more than 2,000 meters (6,500 feet) high.

Ross Ice Shelf: the largest ice shelf in Antarctica. It is joined to the coast of Antarctica.

Ross Sea: a large sea that is partly frozen. The partly frozen area is called the Ross Ice Shelf.

Weddell Sea: a sea named after a man who hunted seals in this area.

Bellingshausen Sea: a sea named after a man who was sent by the Czar (king) of Russia to explore Antarctica.

South Georgia: a subantarctic island close to the southern tip of South America.

Macquarie Island: a subantarctic island that is now a wildlife sanctuary.

Southern Ocean: the ocean that surrounds Antarctica and the subantarctic islands.

A place of extremes

The Antarctic is a place of extremes. For half the year at the South Pole, it is always light. For the other half of the year it is always dark. The Antarctic is also the coldest, driest and windiest place on Earth.

Long days and nights

The South Pole has six months of daytime followed by six months of nighttime each year. The reason for this is due to the tilt of the Earth as it moves around the Sun. From September 23 to March 21, the southern part of the Earth is tilted towards the Sun. This means that the South Pole gets lots of sunlight. From March 21 to September 23, the southern part of the Earth is tilted away from the Sun. This means that the South Pole does not get any sunlight at all.

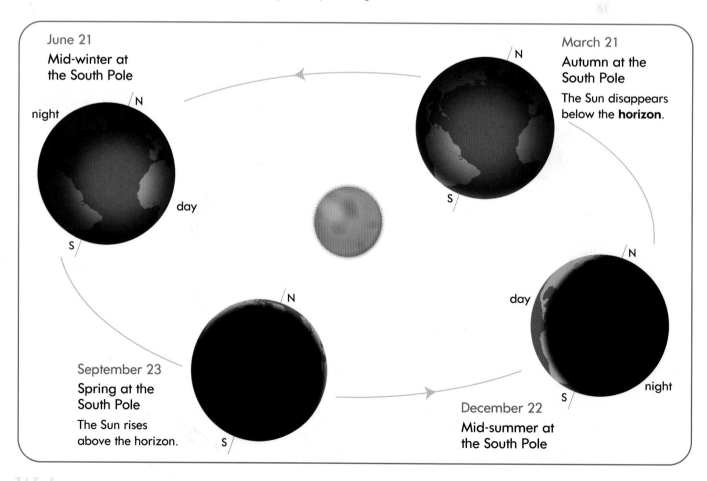

June 21
Mid-winter at the South Pole
night
day

March 21
Autumn at the South Pole
The Sun disappears below the **horizon**.

September 23
Spring at the South Pole
The Sun rises above the horizon.

December 22
Mid-summer at the South Pole
day
night

Climate and weather

Antarctica is the coldest place on earth. In the middle of Antarctica, temperatures usually fall well below minus 40 degrees Celsius (-40° F) in winter and only rise to about minus 25 degrees Celsius (-13° F) in summer. The areas around the coast of Antarctica are usually warmer, with temperatures of around minus 20 degrees Celsius (-4° F) in winter and about 0 degrees Celsius (32° F), or freezing point, in summer.

Antarctica is also the driest place on earth. It is a cold desert. It never rains in Antarctica because it is too cold. Any rain that falls, freezes and forms snowflakes before it reaches the Earth's surface.

Antarctica is also the windiest place on Earth. Strong, cold winds rush down from the middle of Antarctica to the coast. Howling storms called **blizzards** are common. During blizzards, heavy, swirling snow and wind speeds of up to 150 kilometers (93 miles) an hour make it impossible to see.

≋ The weather can change very quickly in the Antarctic. A beautiful calm day can soon turn into a howling blizzard.

Did you know?

The lowest temperature ever recorded on Earth was minus 89.2 degrees Celsius (-129° F) at the Russian station of Vostok near the center of Antarctica.

Snow and ice

The Antarctic is ruled by snow and ice. Most of Antarctica is covered by thick ice caps and glaciers. Ice shelves, **pack ice** and icebergs are all found in the Southern Ocean.

Ice caps

Ice caps are thick layers of ice and snow that cover most of the land of Antarctica. The ice caps have taken thousands of years to build up.

Glaciers

Glaciers are like frozen rivers of ice that move slowly down valleys toward the ocean. Glaciers flow slowly at rates of 10 to 100 meters (32 to 328 feet) per year. Once the glaciers reach the ocean, large blocks of ice break off into the sea as icebergs. This is called **calving**.

≋ A large glacier slides off Antarctica into the sea. Close by are icebergs that have calved off the main glacier.

Water Worlds

Ice shelves

Ice shelves are thick sheets of sea ice joined to the coast of Antarctica. Sometimes ice shelves float in the water and sometimes they rest on the sea-bed.

Pack ice

As winter becomes colder, the ocean surface near Antarctica freezes into a solid sheet of ice called pack ice. Pack ice can be from one to several meters thick. Sometimes strong winds and ocean currents break pack ice into large pieces called **ice floes**.

Icebergs

Icebergs are large blocks of ice that float in the ocean. They break off or calve from the ends of glaciers and sea ice. Some icebergs can be up to 1,000 kilometers (620 miles) long, 20 kilometers (12 miles) wide and 800 meters (2,625 feet) thick. These large icebergs look like floating mountains.

Only about 20 percent of an iceberg shows above the ocean surface. This part is called the **freeboard**. The other 80 percent of an iceberg is below the ocean surface. This part is called the **cold core** because the ice is very cold and heavy.

The most common icebergs in the Antarctic are called **tabular** icebergs. They are shaped like large, table-topped ice cubes.

≋ These blue icebergs floating off the coast of Antarctica have been eroded by the wind to form amazing shapes.

Did you know?

Some icebergs are green because of tiny plants called **algae** growing in the ice.

≋ Ships bring supplies to scientists and visitors staying in Antarctica. They are specially built to be able to break through thick pack ice. In front of the ship, on the pack ice, are some Emperor Penguins.

Living in the Antarctic

The Antarctic can be divided into four parts depending on where living things stay, breed and feed:

- Antarctica
- the Antarctic coast
- the Southern Ocean
- subantarctic islands.

Few living things can survive in the middle of the harsh land of Antarctica. More living things make their home on the coast of Antarctica or on the sea ice around the edges of the land. Some living things inhabit the cold waters of the Southern Ocean, while many living things occupy the warmer subantarctic islands.

≋ A pair of Wandering Albatrosses are nesting on the subantarctic island of South Georgia.

Antarctic birds

There are many different kinds of birds that live and visit the Antarctic.

All Antarctic birds, except penguins, can fly. Some birds, such as terns, only fly in to the Antarctic for the summer. Other birds, such as Wandering Albatrosses, stay all year round and breed on subantarctic islands.

Wandering Albatrosses are the world's largest flying bird. They have a wing span of more than four meters (13 feet). Their big wings allow them to glide great distances over the ocean's surface. Albatrosses feed on fish and squid. They never land on the ocean surface to feed because they are too big and heavy to take off again. Instead, they just swoop down and pluck food from the sea.

≋ This rusty old digester on a subantarctic island called Macquarie Island was once used to cook up dead penguins and seals for their oil.

Did you know?

*Whales, seals and penguins are able to survive in the cold water of the Southern Ocean because they have a thick layer of fat beneath their skin called **blubber**. People used to kill these animals for their blubber. Chunks of blubber would be cooked in huge oven-like machines called digesters. As the blubber was heated, it would melt to form oil. This oil was used to make products such as lipstick and ointments.*

Life on Antarctica

Most of Antarctica is buried under thick ice caps. The parts of Antarctica not covered by ice caps are called **dry valleys**. The largest set of dry valleys are called the McMurdo Dry Valleys. Most of Antarctica's plants and animals live in these dry valleys or close to the coast. However, very few plants and animals live in Antarctica all year round because it is too cold.

Plants

Antarctica is too cold, dry and windy for many types of plants to survive. Only simple plants such as algae, mosses, liverworts and lichens (say: ly-kens) can grow in Antarctica's harsh conditions.

In dry valleys, some rocks have brightly colored lichens growing over them. Lichens are a mixture of fungi (plant-like living things that do not have any color, stems, roots or leaves) and algae (plants with color but without stems, roots or leaves). Lichens survive in Antarctica because they get their food and water directly from the air, and because they grow close to the ground and are sheltered from the wind.

≋ A splash of bright yellow lichen grows over bare rock in a dry valley in Antarctica.

Animals

The only animals that live on Antarctica are small **invertebrates** (say: in-ver-ter-braitz). Invertebrates are animals without backbones. The largest land invertebrates on Antarctica are called midges. They are about 12 millimeters (one-half inch) long and look like wingless flies. The smallest invertebrates, called protozoans (say: pro-toe-zoe-ans), are too small to see.

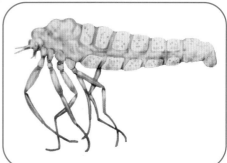

≋ This is a midge. It is the largest animal that lives on Antarctica.

≋ Low-growing moss and lichen are the main types of plants that survive in Antarctica.

Did you know?

Only two percent of Antarctica is not covered by snow and ice.

Life around the Antarctic coast

In winter, part of the Southern Ocean around the coast of Antarctica freezes over, creating large flat areas of ice called pack ice. Some of this ice stays frozen for the whole year and forms ice shelves. Many different types of animals live on this ice and most of them get their food from the ocean.

Seals

Seals belong to a group of animals called **mammals**. Mammals feed their babies with milk. Baby seals are called pups.

There are six different types of seals that live in the Antarctic. Crabeater Seals, Weddell Seals, Ross Seals and Leopard Seals breed on the coast of Antarctica and on the pack ice. Antarctic Fur Seals and Southern Elephant Seals mostly breed on subantarctic islands. All of these types of seals hunt for food in the Southern Ocean.

≋ Weddell Seals are often seen in large groups on pack ice around the coast of Antarctica.

A Leopard Seal looks out from a hole in the pack ice. Behind the seal is a group of Adelie Penguins.

Leopard Seals

Leopard Seals have dark spots on their fur like a leopard. They are strong, fast swimmers and have powerful jaws and sharp teeth. Leopard Seals are good hunters and feed mostly on penguins, fish or smaller seals such as young Crabeaters. Leopard Seals hunt penguins by waiting in the ocean off ice shelves where there are groups of penguins. When the penguins go into the ocean to feed, the Leopard Seals strike. They can skin and eat a penguin with one shake of their head.

Did you know?

Crabeater Seals do not feed on crabs. They feed on small shrimp-like sea animals called krill.

Crabeater Seals are the most common seals in Antarctica.

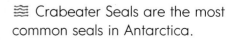

Penguins

Penguins are the most common type of bird in the Antarctic. Penguins do not fly. They use their wings to swim through the ocean when hunting for food. They can dive to depths of up to 60 meters (200 feet) and swim at speeds of up to 40 kilometers (25 miles) an hour. They can stay under the water for more than 15 minutes without breathing.

≋ Emperor Penguins breed on the ice of Antarctica. This chick huddles on the feet of its parent to keep off the freezing ice.

Emperor Penguins

Emperor Penguins are the heaviest and largest of all the penguins. They can grow up to 1.2 meters (4 feet) tall and weigh up to 32 kilograms (70 pounds). Emperor Penguins live in large groups of up to 100,000 birds. These groups are called rookeries. Emperor Penguins are the only penguins to spend the winter on the pack ice.

In mid-May, female Emperor Penguins lay a single egg. Male Emperor Penguins scoop up the egg and place it on their feet. Then they cover it with a flap of skin to keep it warm. The females then leave to spend most of the winter feeding in the ocean. The males stay behind to look after the eggs.

The males huddle together to help survive the cold, windy winter. During this time, the males do not feed and lose almost half their body weight. In July, just as the eggs hatch, female Emperor Penguins return and take over from the males. From then on, Emperor Penguins share the care of their chick. By mid-December the chicks are big enough to survive on their own.

Did you know?

Emperor Penguins can live for 20 to 30 years.

🌊 An Adelie Penguin walks through an ice cave on the coast of Antarctica.

Adelie Penguins

Adelie Penguins live and breed on the coastal areas of Antarctica and on the pack ice. They feed on fish and krill. Male Adelie Penguins arrive before the females on the coast of Antarctica in spring and begin building nests. The female Adelie Penguins reach them a few days later. In spring, female Adelie Penguins usually lay two eggs. The eggs take about 35 days to hatch.

During this time, the parents take turns keeping the eggs warm and going off to feed in the ocean.

After the eggs hatch, the chicks stay close to their parents for about three weeks. When the chicks are three weeks old, the parents leave the chicks by themselves and only return to feed them krill, small fish and squid until they are big enough to feed themselves.

Life in the Southern Ocean

The Southern Ocean is the coldest ocean in the world. It surrounds Antarctica and the subantarctic islands. The water of the Southern Ocean is home to many different sorts of animals such as small sea animals, fishes and whales.

Krill

Krill are invertebrates with 10 legs. They look like small see-through prawns. Female krill lay eggs twice during the summer. Each time they can lay as many as 2,000 to 3,000 eggs. These eggs are carried by deep ocean currents to the edge of the Antarctic continent. Here, the eggs hatch and the young krill begin to grow. After two or three years, the adult krill rise to the ocean's surface. They form huge groups that cover hundreds of miles of the Southern Ocean. They are an important source of food for many different kinds of animals such as fishes, whales, seals, penguins and other sea birds.

Did you know?

Krill use their legs to make a net to catch tiny plants and animals to eat.

≋ Antarctic krill are an important source of food for many Antarctic animals.

≋ Antarctic fish look very strange, but they are able to survive the cold waters of the Southern Ocean.

Antarctic fishes

While there are about 15,000 different types of fishes found in all the oceans around the world, there are only about 200 types of fishes found in the ocean around Antarctica. This is because only some fishes, such as icefishes, can survive the Southern Ocean's freezing waters. Antarctic fishes have developed a kind of antifreeze in their bodies that stops their body fluids freezing. Some Antarctic fishes have white blood rather than red blood. Scientists are not sure how this helps their survival. They think it has something to do with making their blood freeze at lower temperatures.

Whales

Whales are mammals that live in the ocean. They must come to the surface of the ocean to breathe air. Whales are divided into two groups:

- toothed whales, such as Sperm Whales and Killer Whales;
- baleen whales such as Blue Whales and Humpback Whales.

Humpback Whales

Humpback Whales are a type of baleen whale. Baleen whales have comb-like fringes of material called baleen hanging from their upper jaws. Humpback Whales use baleen to strain krill and other small invertebrates from the ocean. They feed in groups called **pods**. One pod can have as many as 25 whales in it.

Did you know?

Killer Whales are fierce hunters. They work together with other Killer Whales to trap and eat seals, penguins and other small whales.

≋ Tourists in a rubber dinghy take a closer look at a pod of Humpback Whales.

Life on subantarctic islands

Subantarctic islands, such as South Georgia and Macquarie Island, are dotted throughout the Southern Ocean. Many plants and animals, including humans, live on and visit subantarctic islands because they are warmer than the rest of the Antarctic.

≋ Low-growing plants called Macquarie Island Cabbages grow on the cliffs of Macquarie Island.

Plants

More plants grow on subantarctic islands than on Antarctica. There are no trees on subantarctic islands. There are just small shrubs, grasses and low-growing plants, such as mosses and lichens, in areas where there is no ice. On many of the islands, there is very little soil for plants to grow in and use as food. Often, the places where plants grow best are close to penguin or seal colonies. Here, the animals' droppings improve the poor soils and provide extra food for plants.

Animals

Birds such as Macaroni Penguins, King Penguins and Royal Penguins live and breed on subantarctic islands. Other seabirds, such as Arctic Terns, fly down from the far north to spend the summer breeding in the Antarctic. Southern Elephant Seals and Antarctic Fur Seals gather in huge numbers to breed on the islands' beaches.

≋ Macaroni Penguins have yellow eye crests. Their eggs hatch in early December on the subantarctic island of South Georgia.

Did you know?

Southern Elephant Seals have a sack of skin on their nose that looks like a small trunk. They use this trunk to make a loud roar to frighten other seals away.

≋ Southern Elephant Seals are the largest Antarctic seal. Males can grow up to seven meters (23 feet) long and weigh up to four tons. Here, two are lying in front of an old whaling station called Grytviken on the subantarctic island of South Georgia.

Food web of the Antarctic

A food web shows what the different living things in a habitat eat. The food web below shows the feeding links between animals that live in the Southern Ocean. If any of the links are harmed or taken away, many animals in the food web will be affected. Plants are the beginning of all food webs. One group of plants that live in the Southern Ocean are tiny, simple plants called algae.

Herbivores (say: her-bi-vorz) are animals that eat plants. For example, some krill eat plants.

Carnivores (say: kar-ni-vorz) are animals that eat other animals. For example, Humpback Whales eat krill.

Sun

algae

krill

small fishes and squid

large fishes

Blue Whale

Crabeater Seal

Killer Whale

≋ King Penguins look like they are flying underwater. They may be feeding or trying to escape being eaten by a seal.

Did you know?

King Penguins breed in huge colonies on the beaches of subantarctic islands.

seabirds

penguins

Ross Seal

Weddell Seal

Leopard Seal

≋ In a food web, arrows point from the food to the living thing that eats it. For example, some krill eat algae.

Did you know?

Food webs can be disturbed by natural events such as storms. They can also be disturbed by human causes such as pollution.

Protecting and studying the Antarctic

No one country owns Antarctica. Antarctica is shared between several countries who have agreed to a set of rules, called the Antarctic Treaty.

≋ A map of Antarctica showing the sectors claimed by different countries.

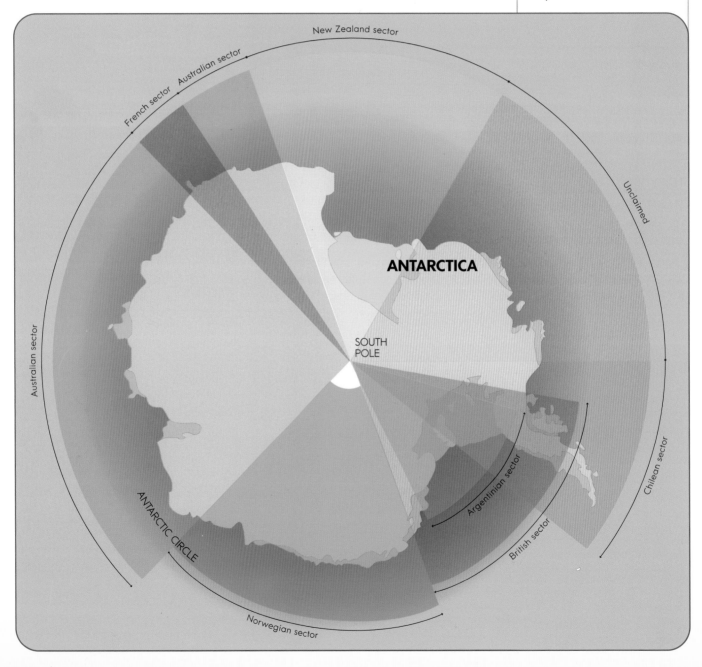

New Zealand sector

French sector

Australian sector

Unclaimed

Australian sector

ANTARCTICA

SOUTH POLE

ANTARCTIC CIRCLE

Chilean sector

Argentinian sector

British sector

Norwegian sector

The Antarctic Treaty

The Antarctic Treaty helps to protect and conserve the plants, animals and environments of Antarctica. This Treaty allows Antarctica to only be used for peaceful aims such as scientific study. The Treaty stops Antarctica from being mined, used as a nuclear dumping ground or as a war zone. The Antarctic Treaty was signed by 40 countries in 1961 and has recently been updated to include more rules about how Antarctica should be managed.

Discovering the past and telling the future

Each year, a layer of snow is added to the ice caps of Antarctica. By carefully studying the different layers of snow and ice, scientists can work out the age of the ice and what the Earth's climate was like in the past. To do this, scientists drill deep into the ice cap and pull out columns of ice called **ice cores**. By carefully counting the number of ice layers, scientists can work out how old the ice is. Some ice cores are two kilometers (1.2 miles) long and the ice at the bottom of these cores is more than 150,000 years old.

Scientists also study the chemicals contained in the different layers of ice. These chemicals tell them the temperatures of past climates. By comparing the age of the ice layer to the chemicals they contain, scientists can work how hot or cold it was in the past.

Ice cores also show whether today's climate is heating up too much because of **greenhouse gases**. Greenhouse gases, such as carbon dioxide, are made by people burning coal and gas. Greenhouse gases trap the Sun's energy and cause the air to heat up. If the air heats up too much, it could cause the Earth's temperature to rise quickly; this could melt the ice caps of Antarctica.

≋ Today's scientists use motor vehicles instead of dog sleds to pull supplies and equipment.

Did you know?

If all the ice covering Antarctica melted, the level of all the world's oceans could rise by up to 200 meters (656 feet). This would flood many low-lying countries.

≋ Scientists are taking samples of ice from various depths to find out more about the past climate of Antarctica.

Ozone

When sunlight shines on a chemical in the air called oxygen, it changes the oxygen into another chemical called **ozone**. Ozone is important because it helps stop harmful rays from the Sun getting through to the Earth's surface. Ozone builds up in a blanket-like layer, about 10 to 30 kilometers (six to 18 miles) above the Earth's surface.

Since the 1970s, scientists have been worried about the ozone layer for two reasons: first, because it has become thinner and second, because it develops a hole in it every spring over Antarctica. Each year scientists measure the size of the ozone hole to see if it has gotten bigger or smaller. Unfortunately, it has become bigger.

Scientists think the hole has been caused by human-made chemicals that destroy ozone. These chemicals are called **chlorofluorocarbons** (say: klor-roe-floo-roe-kar-benz) and were used in fridges and aerosol cans. Recently many countries, including Australia, passed laws to stop the use of chlorofluorocarbons. Even so, scientists believe that it will take a long time for the ozone layer to recover.

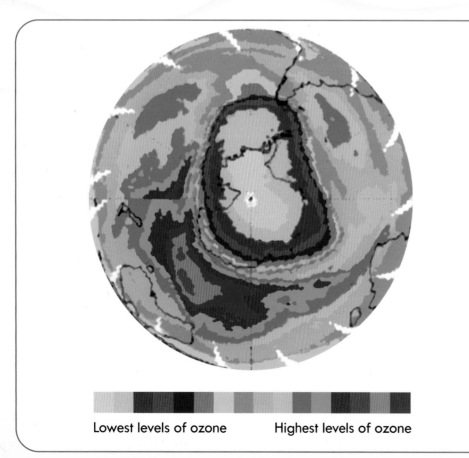

≋ This map shows the low levels of ozone over the Antarctic in September, 1998.

Lowest levels of ozone   Highest levels of ozone

The Antarctic sky

The Antarctic sky is of great interest to scientists. Many scientists study the strange pink and green lights that flash across the sky during winter as well as the layers of protective chemicals found high up in the sky.

Lights in the sky

On clear, cold nights, pink and green lights flicker across the skies of the Antarctic. The lights are called the Aurora Australis or the southern lights. The lights are caused by the solar wind (which is a stream of particles made by the Sun) bumping into the chemicals that make air. When they bump together, they make colored lights between 70 and 200 kilometers (44 and 124 miles) above the Earth's surface.

The Aurora Australis is especially bright after solar flares. Solar flares are huge explosions that take place on the Sun's surface. These explosions make the solar wind very strong which, in turn, makes the lights very bright.

Did you know?

The **Maori** people of New Zealand call the Aurora Australis the 'burning of the sky' because the lights in the sky make it look as if the sky is on fire.

≋ The brilliant Aurora Australis lights up an Antarctic winter sky with streaks of pink and green light.

Environment watch

Why is the Antarctic important?

The Antarctic is important for four main reasons:

- It is the largest remaining unspoiled area on Earth.
- Many special plants and animals live there.
- It provides a record showing the changing patterns of Earth's climate and weather.
- There is nowhere else like it on Earth.

Things You Can Do
to help protect the Antarctic

◇ Be interested in what is happening in the Antarctic. Read the newspapers, watch the news and use the Internet to find out what is going on.

◇ Avoid using products containing chlorofluorocarbons.

◇ Cut down on energy use at home. This will reduce the amount of greenhouse gases produced and help to stop the earth heating up too much.

◇ Join a conservation group and help to protect and conserve the plants and animals of the Antarctic.

≋ This hut was once used by Captain Robert Scott, an early explorer of Antarctica. In the background is a modern scientific base called McMurdo station.

Glossary

algae	plants, such as seaweeds, that live in wet conditions and do not have leaves, stems or roots
blizzards	terrible storms with swirling snow and high winds
blubber	a layer of fat below the skin of whales and seals
calving	icebergs breaking away from glaciers or sea ice
chlorofluorocarbons	chemicals made by humans that destroy ozone
cold core	the part of a glacier underneath the surface of the ocean
continent	a large unbroken area of land. There are seven continents: Antarctica, Australia, Asia, Europe, North America, South America and Africa.
dry valleys	large areas of ice-free land on Antarctica
freeboard	the part of an iceberg showing above the surface of the ocean
glacier	frozen rivers of ice
greenhouse gases	gases such as carbon dioxide, which can cause the Earth's temperature to rise
horizon	the line where the land or sea and sky seem to meet
ice cores	columns of ice drilled out of Antarctica's ice cap
ice floes	broken pack ice
ice shelf	a thick sheet of sea ice joined to the coast of Antarctica
icebergs	large blocks of ice that break off glaciers or sea ice into the ocean
invertebrates	groups of animals that do not have a backbone, such as krill, midges and protozoans
mammals	a group of animals that feed their young milk
Maori	the indigenous people of New Zealand
ozone	a chemical that protects the Earth from the harmful rays of the sun
pack ice	thick, solid sheets of ice that form over the ocean's surface in winter
pods	groups of whales
sea ice	a layer of ice that forms on the ocean's surface
tabular	a word to describe an iceberg that is flat like a table top

Index

W9-CDM-988

WITHDRAWN

IMPOSSIBLE
objects

Amazing Optical Illusions to Confound & Astound

J. TIMOTHY UNRUH

STERLING PUBLISHING CO., INC.
New York

This book is dedicated to Jack C. Thomas
who first introduced me to an impossible object
and to John E. Wells
who wholeheartedly shared my enthusiasm.

Library of Congress Cataloging-in-Publication Data Available

Published by Sterling Publishing Company, Inc.
387 Park Avenue South, New York, N.Y. 10016
© 2001 by J. Timothy Unruh
Distributed in Canada by Sterling Publishing
c/o Canadian Manda Group, One Atlantic Avenue, Suite 105
Toronto, Ontario, Canada M6K 3E7
Distributed in Great Britain and Europe by Cassell PLC
Wellington House, 125 Strand, London WC2R 0BB, England
Distributed in Australia by Capricorn Link (Australia) Pty Ltd.
P.O. Box 6651, Baulkham Hills, Business Centre, NSW 2153, Australia

Manufactured in the United States of America
All rights reserved

Sterling ISBN 0-8069-4996-1

CONTENTS

"There's no use trying," Alice said. "One can't believe impossible things."

"I daresay you haven't had much practice," said the Queen. "When I was your age, I always did it for half an hour a day. Why, sometimes I've believed as many as six impossible things before breakfast," the Queen boasted to Alice.

—Lewis Carroll, *Through the Looking Glass* (1872)

INTRODUCTION

im·pos·si·ble (im-pos´e-b´l), *adj.* [ME.; OFr.; L. impossibilis; see IN- (not) & POSSIBLE]: not capable of being . . . or happening . . . .

Optical illusions of one kind or another have been of part of man's experience since the beginning of history. The mirage seen in the desert, the famous moon illusion—where the moon rising over the horizon looks so much larger than when seen high in the sky—the illusions created in light and shadow, and those of relative motion are just a few intriguing examples from the natural world. When these tricks of the eye and mind were first observed, they undoubtedly stirred the imagination. They were something that, upon closer examination, weren't as they appeared to be.

In time, illusions were employed to improve the effectiveness of art forms and the aesthetics of architecture. The ancient Greeks made use of the optical illusion to perfect the appearance of their great temples. In the Middle Ages, misplaced perspective was occasionally incorporated into paintings for practical reasons. In more recent times many more illusions have been created and implemented in the graphic arts. Among these is the unique and fairly new strain of illusion that has become known as the "impossible object."

Basic to our technical training and practice is the ability to perceive real three-dimensional objects in a two-dimensional medium or drawing. Impossible objects involve manipulations of perspective and depth in these two-dimensional media. Impossible in the real three-dimensional world, they function on misplaced perspective; depth inversions; misleading visual cues; discontinuity of planes; ambiguous coverings, shadings, and joinings; false and conflicting orientations and connections; altered vanishing points, and other "tricks" of the graphic artist. All of these techniques involve perspective, which is itself an illusion, because perspective involves nothing more than creating the appearance—or illusion—of depth in three-dimensional space. Looking at it from this point of view, impossible objects are actually double illusions.

As unique products of these unusual techniques, impossible objects captivate the imagination and tantalize us with their mysterious properties. At the same time they illuminate something of our remarkable processes of vision and thought as the mind's eye seeks an integrated solution compatible with everyday reality. As the eye sees and the brain thinks, we are forced to accept a visual conflict that is never encountered in the real world. Of all the optical illusions known, impossible objects are perhaps the most intriguing. The tricks they play on the mind's eye and the playful manner in which they cause extraordinary temporary consternation to the human psyche make them uniquely entertaining.

Impossible objects work contrary to our fundamental notions of perception. For example, when we look at a figure in this book we first perceive a three-dimensional object, but then we sense that something is not quite right. A moment later we realize that the object is spatially impossible, yet we see clearly that it is obviously possible on paper. It is not the two-dimensional representation that is impossible, but the three-dimensional one. In other words, impossible objects represent a sort of netherland of figures that can be imagined and fairly easily drawn, but not constructed in the real world. This is what gives them their fascination and appeal.

Just as important, impossible objects are different from other impossibilities. On one hand, we can imagine a woman with a fish tail—a mermaid; even though, as far as we know, mermaids do not and cannot exist, we have no problem drawing them. On the other hand, we cannot imagine a square circle, nor can we draw such a thing. The discrepancy between "square" and "circle" is so great that they cannot be dealt with simultaneously, hence such a thing is impossible in the world of our imagination as well as in the world of reality. Neither the square nor the circle shares the attribute that is of cardinal importance to the impossible object—the attribute of ambiguity. In an impossible object we may see the ambiguity but we cannot sensibly resolve it in our mind's eye. As we shall see, impossible objects are strangely imaginable.

It has been said of impossible objects that their discreet violations of our most ingrained interpretations of external reality grab us at a deep, mysterious, and unarticulated level. When we look at an impossible object, a vague disquiet moves us to take a closer look. Suddenly, our familiar world, which seems so stable, reliable, and solid, shatters unexpectedly almost as if in a strange dream. As we continue to gaze at the object, which seems to undergo a number of oscillations, our mind finally leads us to the realization that the aberration was only in the mind's eye and not in the real world. In the end, we might say that reality regains its composure and we laugh, as if at a narrowly averted accident!

Drafting Tools of the Impossibler

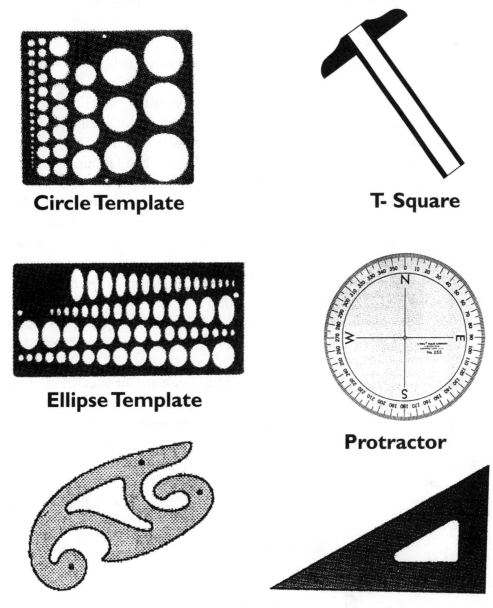

Circle Template

T- Square

Ellipse Template

Protractor

French Curve

30°-60° Triangle

Hey! Wait a Minute! That's Impossible!

THE deliberate design of impossible objects has its counterpart in earlier times, before the age of classical perspective, when artists found solutions by bending the rules imposed by convention. An example of such a "fudging" was found in artwork dating from the 15th century, depicting the Annunciation on a fresco in St. Mary's Cathedral in Breda, Holland. The scene shows the Archangel Gabriel bringing tidings to Mary of her future Son. It is framed by two slightly pointed arches, which are in turn supported by three columns. However, the point of interest is the middle column. Unlike the left and right columns, which are in the foreground, the middle column disappears into the background behind a table. The practical reason for this "impossibility" was its use as a strategy to avoid splitting the scene into two separate halves.

The impossible object shown on the facing page bears a resemblance to the arch-column configuration in this mural at Breda. Here a flat wall exists in two different pictorial planes and the result is what we call a "planar discontinuity." Thus, the impossible object as we know it has existed for at least 500 years!

The impossible objects that appear in this book are for you, the reader, to enjoy as you explore this intriguing new world. As you journey through them you will find that perhaps—and just perhaps—you will be able to imagine and create your very own entirely new impossible objects! Most of the figures in this book were discovered this way. Impossibiliting like this is truly great fun!

J. Timothy Unruh
Rocklin, California

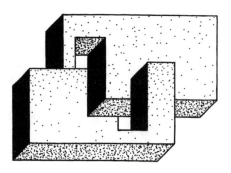

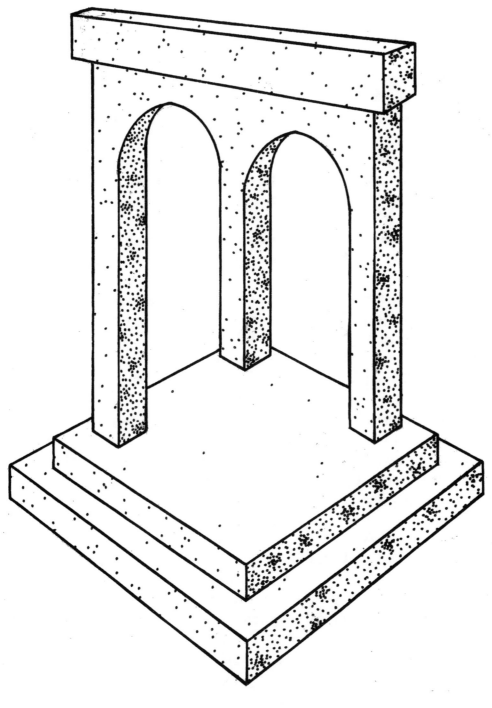

AN EARLY IMPOSSIBLE OBJECT

PART I

The Impossible Triangle—The Tribar

THIS figure is probably the first formally published example of an impossible object. It appeared in the *British Journal of Psychology* in an article titled "Impossible Objects, a Special Type of Visual Illusion" in 1958. The authors, Lionel and Roger Penrose, father and son, a geneticist and mathematician respectively, referred to it as a "three-dimensional rectangular structure." It has also been called a "tribar" or a "warped tribar." Two other intriguing figures were also featured in the article. Thus, with these three, the "impossible object" was formally introduced into public awareness.

Soon afterward, the late and now very popular Dutch surrealist artist Maurits C. Escher (1898–1972) discovered the Penrose Triangle. At the time, he had just begun to be engrossed with the construction of impossible worlds. Subsequently, the Penrose Triangle, or the tribar, became the inspiration for Escher's extremely successful 1961 lithograph "Waterfall," which incorporated a clever linking of three tribars. In his drawing Escher essentially created a visually convincing perpetual-motion machine. It was perpetual in that it provided an endless watercourse along a circuit formed by the three linked triangles. Anyone who has been in a store where books and posters are sold has probably seen this image. Not only Escher but many others have copied and republished the tribar in their own varied forms, building upon the work that came before. The tribar is the first of the four great classic types of impossible objects, the others being the "Endless Staircase," the "Space Fork," and the "Crazy Crate."

When you first view the tribar, it looks like a simple drawing of an equilateral triangle. However, upon closer inspection, you see that there is something rather uncanny about it. The bars meeting at the top of the drawing appear to be perpendicular, while the bars at the lower left and lower right also appear to be perpendicular. Each corner presents a different angle to your eye. The triangle, or whatever you want to call it, is logically consistent in each of its individual areas, but is nonsensical overall. It is not truly warped, but only held together as a drawing through the incorrect connections of normal elements.

THE TRIBAR

Triple Warped Tribar

THE figure at the right is a simple but profound elaboration of the Penrose Triangle. That tribar exhibited a single impossibility, while this figure has many. As your eye examines this figure—as with any impossible object—you must reappraise the drawing at every turn. The object has a convincing solidity, but if you tried to build such a thing it just wouldn't work out. This is at the essence of impossible objects!

TRIPLE WARPED TRIBAR

Twelve-Cube Triangle

GEOMETRIC shapes are the best sources of inspiration for developing impossible objects. Take the simple cube, for instance. We see thousands of them in one form or another every day. As you can easily see in the figure on the facing page, we took one of the tribars from a previous page and broke it down into cubes. By doing that nothing was lost: this figure is just as profoundly impossible as its predecessor!

Constructed of a dozen cubes, this arrangement was laid out on a drafts-man's board with a plastic 30°/60° triangle. The drafting triangle was useful in making sure that the individual cubes conformed to the overall perspective of the drawing. The impossibility, which takes advantage of this perspective, is accomplished by the false foreground-background placement of the rows of cubes, an effect similar to the one in the tribar. In other words, the drawing is held together through the incorrect connections of the normal rows of cubes.

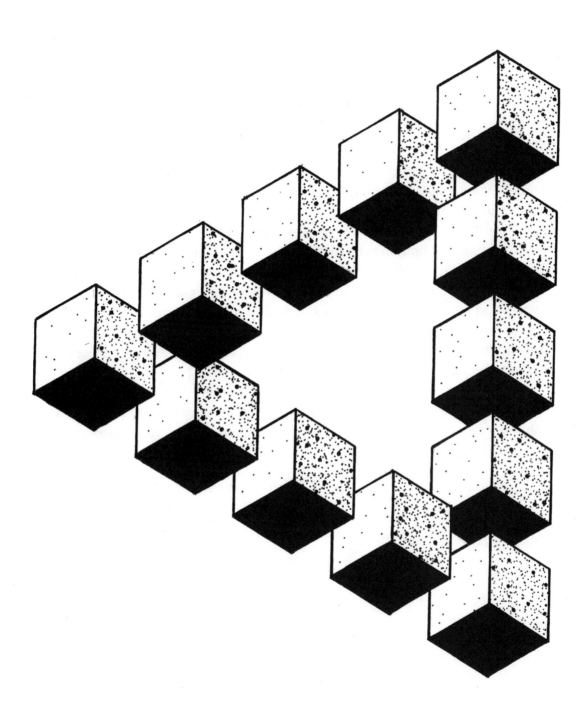

TWELVE-CUBE TRIANGLE

Winged Tribar

THE "Winged Tribar" on page 17 is another elaboration of the tribar concept, which just goes to show how easy it is to create unique and intriguing new variations on a single theme. The tribar lends itself to many interesting variations!

For years psychologists have employed geometric figures of various sorts in their studies of human personality and behavior. Since the turn of the century more than 200 figures and illusions have been devised in order to analyze the psychology of seeing and the process of eye-brain dynamics of patients as they view these objects and attempt to make sense of them. Many insights about personality types have been derived from such experiments where incompatible information is given to the eye. A few of these figures even include impossible objects like this one.

It's interesting to watch someone viewing an impossible figure, and certainly entertaining to observe them trying to make sense of it. Impossible objects seem to be useful tools for psychologists in their quest to find out what makes people tick.

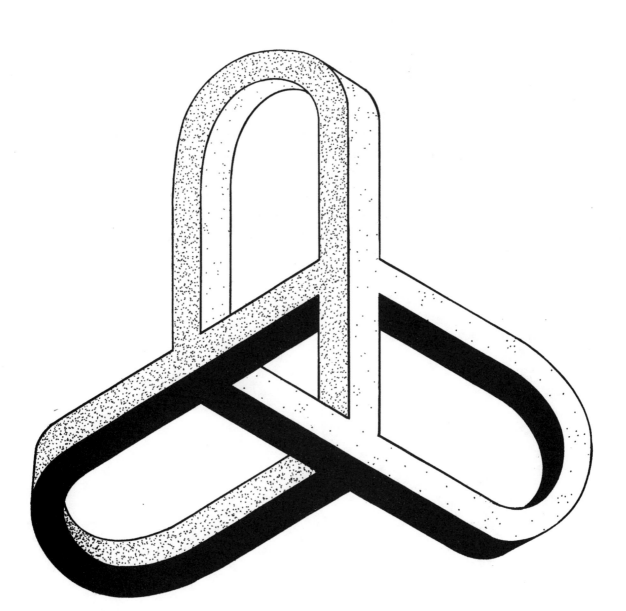

WINGED TRIBAR

Tri-Domino

To accomplish what this three-piece suite appears to demonstrate would normally require four elements, not just three. Try it yourself the next time you play dominoes! To make a normal circle you need 360 degrees, but this object seems to close the 360-degree loop in just 270 degrees! Upon closer examination, it becomes apparent that this figure operates on a misplaced return in perspective—similar to that of the impossible tribar. This figure is really merely an impossible tribar in which the three perimeter elements have been replaced by the familiar game pieces.

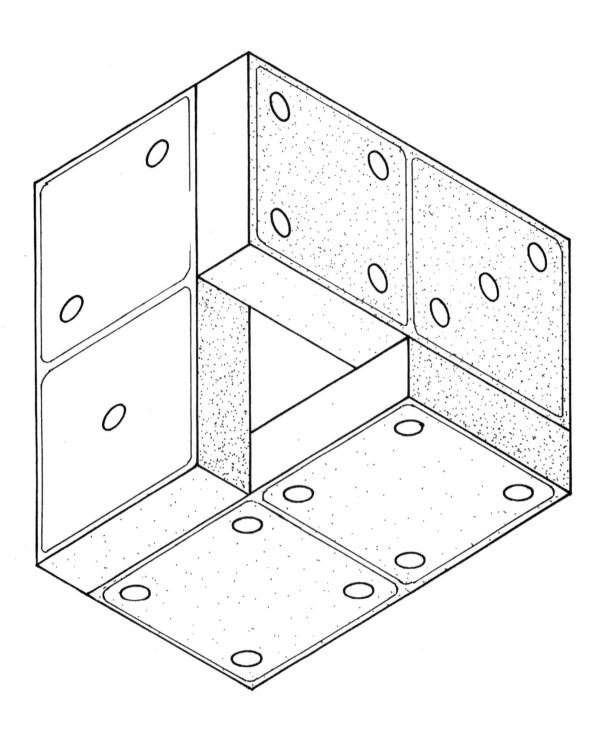

TRI-DOMINO

Dowel Block

THE more sophisticated version of the tribar principle, shown on the facing page, was inspired by a child's building block and a Tinkertoy™. This object consists of a pair of complementary dowel-like components that penetrate the block and then intersect outside the block at an impossible juncture. It is the juncture alone that makes this impossible object possible, at least on paper! That this profound figure is a triangle is evident even in this simple two-element composition.

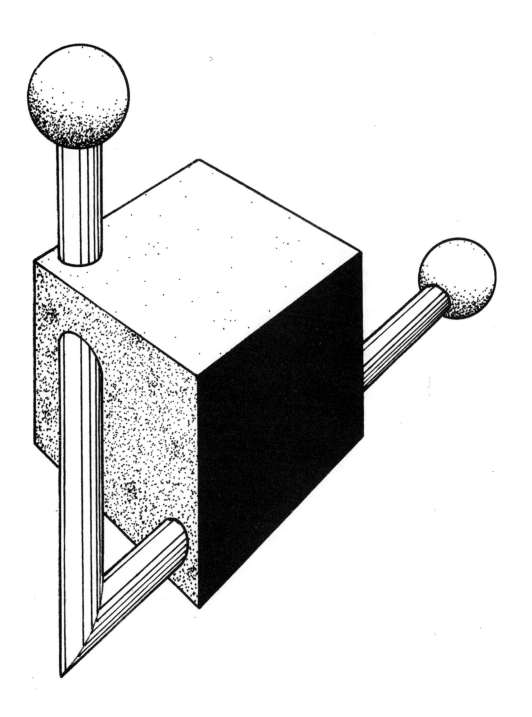

DOWEL BLOCK

Truncated Tribar

As we become more closely acquainted with the tribar and its seemingly limitless expressions, we now find a new and curious variation.

The "Truncated Tribar" is simply a tribar with one corner chopped off—"truncated." As a result the figure now has four sides. If this object were a window, what a job it would be to install the glass pane! (It would be a real pain!)

As with the impossible tribar, our eye accepts it as a solid object at first glance, but then sees it as a sort of window frame. It cannot really exist, of course, but then again it is a figure we cannot easily dismiss. The effectiveness of the "Truncated Tribar" illusion arises from a combination of misplaced perspective and false connections.

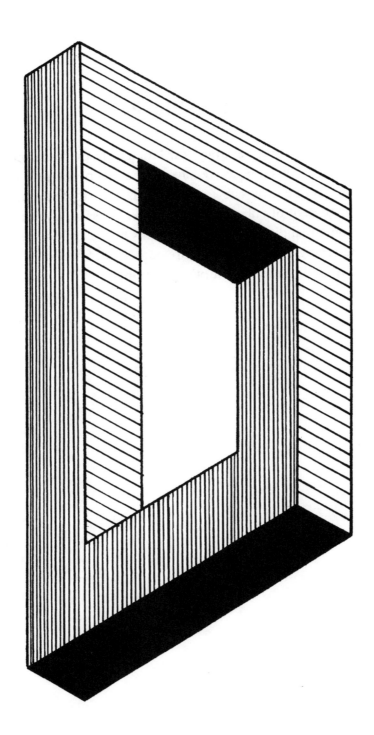

TRUNCATED TRIBAR

Mental Blocks

CHILDREN'S blocks? Computer graphics? No, it's another version of the impossible tribar! The cube, as we have already seen, is a very useful element in constructing impossible objects. This is a simple but intriguing triangular arrangement of cubes. It functions on the same dynamics as its ancestor. The only real differences between this figure and the previous "Twelve-Cube Triangle" is that this figure consists of fewer cubes and provides a mentally challenging and subtle variation.

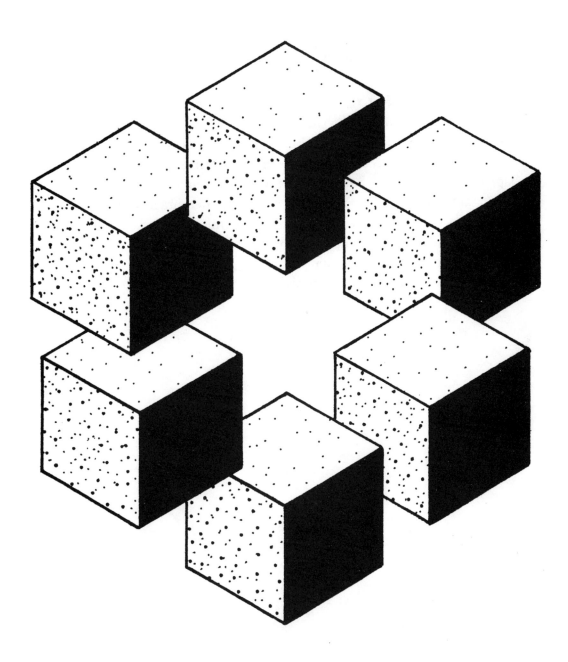

MENTAL BLOCKS

Diamond Crossover

THE enigmatic figure on the facing page was derived from staring at a cross-truss that supported a stair landing at a two-level apartment complex. Again, the principle of the tribar is quite evident. The "Diamond Crossover" is essentially nothing more than two tribars glued together in the shape of a diamond. You could expand on this design by gluing together additional tribars here. As mentioned earlier, Escher attached three tribars in his famous composition. There really is no limit. In fact, you could glue many such tribars together in a pattern that would be very effective in a pieced quilt or some other design. Otherwise, we leave it to you, the observer, to triangulate this squeamish, squashed, squarish thing!

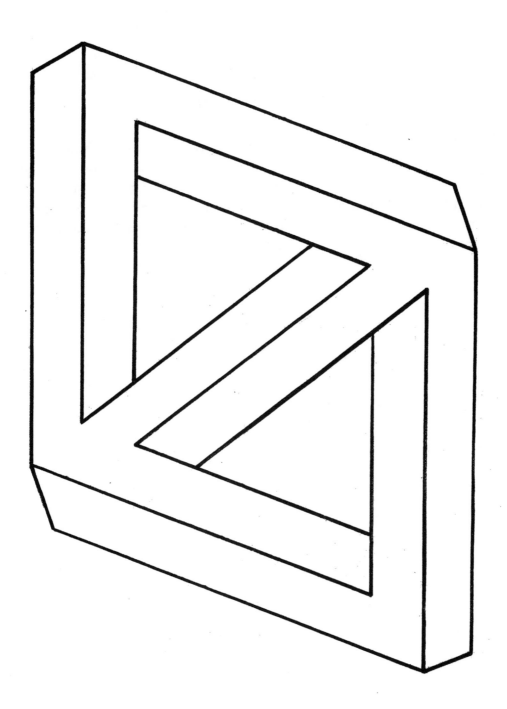

DIAMOND CROSSOVER

Mounted Tribar

THIS figure is an instant replay, with more variations, of the infamous tribar. This time the object is placed appropriately (yet impossibly) on its own rack for public display. Because of its odd interface between reality and fantasy, this object seems to peel away and float over, or hover slightly above, its pedestal! The additional floating illusion is an effect of its depth ambiguity.

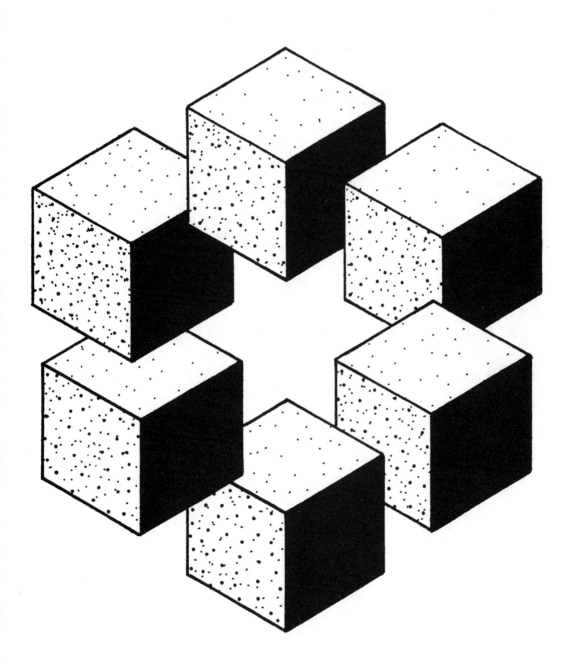

MOUNTED TRIBAR

Warped Tribar Truncate

THE "Warped Tribar Truncate" is, in essence, another chopped-off, or truncated, tribar with some internal variation. It looks as if it could be a surrealist design for a new style of furniture, but would certainly stop cold any carpenter who accepted an order for a dozen of these things. Then again, this piece of very expressive mini-art could open up a host of new ideas for everything from lawn chairs to plaza sculptures!

The visual arts cater to a wide variety of human needs. Impossible objects, like this one, present an amusing interplay of intrigue and entertainment. They could be called "recreational art"!

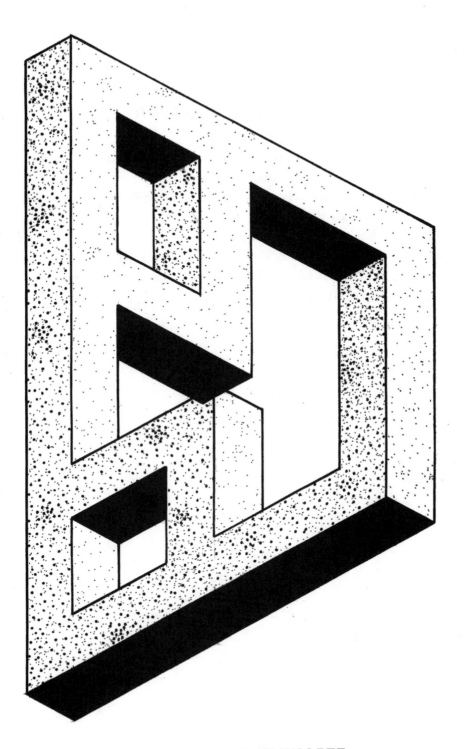

WARPED TRIBAR TRUNCATE

Ethereal Hexagon

THIS rich new variation of the tribar, based on symmetry and repetition, is a design reminiscent of an image one might see in a kaleidoscope. You will notice that the grand underlying principle of the tribar is incorporated into this innovative design.

Like the other tribars, this one is relatively easy to create. It looks as though all you need is a potter's wheel to turn the drawing so that you can make all the extremities identical. It is easy to see that this figure, like all tribar figures, is based on a triangle.

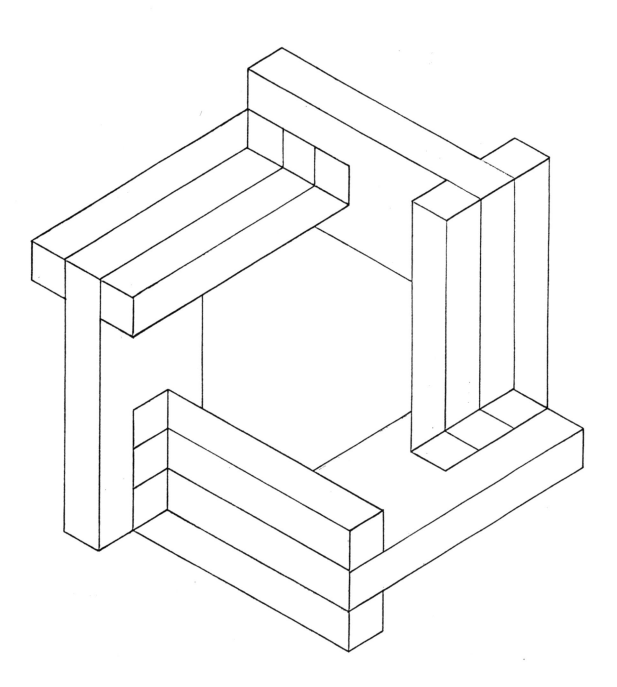

ETHEREAL HEXAGON

Rectangular Trihedron

IN this concluding example of the tribar theme, we see yet another intriguing way to elaborate on the Penrose Triangle. In case you're wondering if the tribar model is now exhausted, rest assured that new ideas will always be coming up—that's guaranteed!

In principle, this figure functions very much like the other members of the tribar family. It is basically a three-dimensional equilateral triangle made up of rectangular solids that cause your gaze to dance about from one extremity to the other in an attempt to make sense out of the figure.

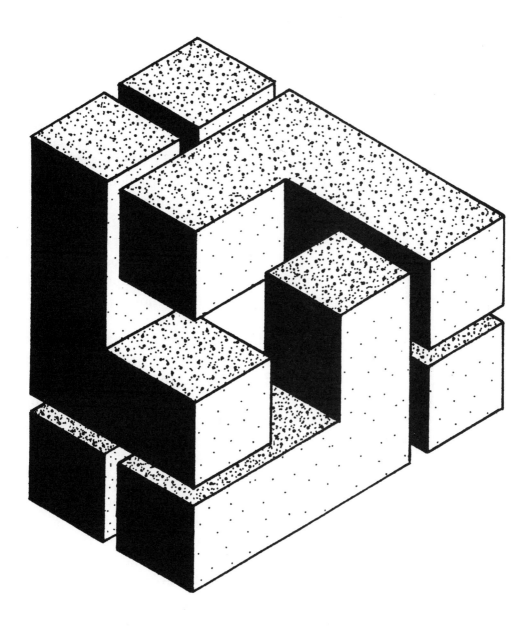

RECTANGULAR TRIHEDRON

PART II
The Endless Staircase

ONE of the best known of the great classics of Impossibilia, this figure is known most often as the "Endless Staircase." It has also been called the "Everlasting" or "Infinite Staircase" or the "Penrose Staircase," after its originators. It has also been referred to as "a continually ascending or descending path."

This figure was first published in 1958 by Lionel and Roger Penrose along with the tribar and another illusion in the *British Journal of Psychology*. In this illusion you are confronted with a stairway said to lead upward or downward without getting any higher or lower. On completion of one visual circuit, you find yourself back where you started. If you were to actually walk this stairway, you would find yourself uselessly ascending or descending into infinity and getting a great deal of exercise. You might call it the ultimate treadmill! Since the Penroses first published it, this impossible object has probably appeared in print more often than any other impossible object. You'll find it in books on games, puzzles, illusions, psychology, and other subjects as well.

The "Endless Staircase" was another figure put to great use by Maurits C. Escher, this time in his fascinating 1960 lithograph "Ascending and Descending." In his graphic, which explored the Penrose artifact to its fullest potential, the very recognizable "Endless Staircase" is neatly set into the rooftop of a monastery, on which a number of hooded monks of an unknown sect march perpetually clockwise and counterclockwise, passing each other as they continue in opposite directions around their impossible rooftop conveyance, never really managing to go up or down. Consequently the staircase has become more associated with Escher, who copied it, than the Penroses, who originated it.

A few years ago researchers at the Bell Telephone Laboratory produced a film featuring the "Endless Staircase." It shows a ball bounding endlessly in a circuit on top of the staircase. To enhance the effectiveness of this illusion a musical note sounds at each bounce and rises in pitch with each step up, but beyond the scale of a single octave the notes never seem to get any higher. After a number of steps up there is a pause, and then the next tone drops an octave but the brain fails to realize it. The ball and the music added to the "Endless Staircase" result in a most convincing and eerie, doubly impossible audiovisual illusion.

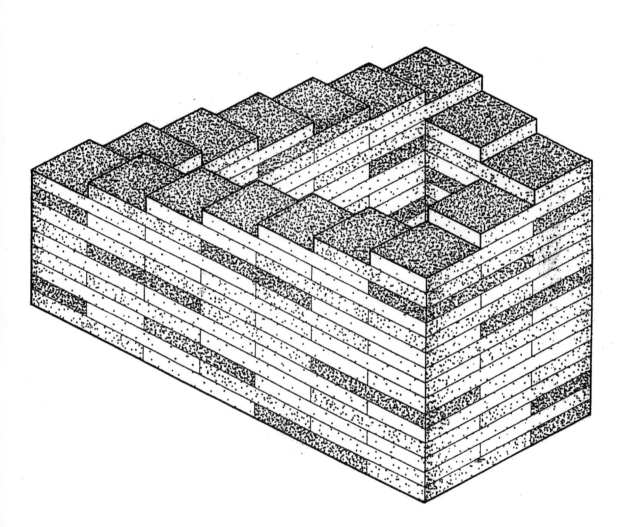

ENDLESS STAIRCASE

Ambiguous Curb-Stepway

AT first glance the "Ambiguous Curb-Stepway" appears as a whole and complete entity. But then upon closer inspection you become aware that there is a serious incongruity. The contradiction becomes most apparent when you alternately cover the left two-thirds, and then the right two-thirds, of the drawing. For example, cover the curb at the upper left while leaving the stepped wall at the lower right exposed, then cover the lower right of the figure, leaving most of the curb end exposed. This "silent interrogation" is a quick and easy demonstration of the object's impossibility! Unlike its cousin the "Endless Staircase," where the primary attribute is the perpetual ascending or descending steps, the "Ambiguous Curb-Stepway" functions on a conflict of planes. The steps seem to emerge out of a single plane in an effect we might call a dual discontinuity.

It would seem easy enough to climb the steps up to the top on the right side of the object and then start walking along the plane toward the left, but then you find yourself back on the bottom again! However, during the walk, be careful lest you fall off into oblivion, or tumble into the stream of space below the left end of the curb. In such an ambiguous "cross-dimensional" fringe reality as this, anything can happen!

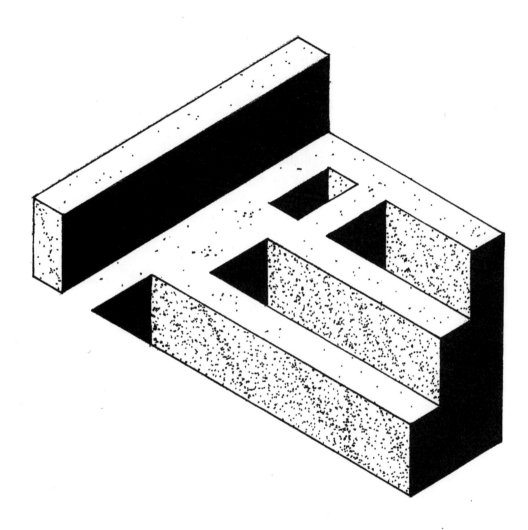

AMBIGUOUS CURB-STEPWAY

Four-Seven Stick Stack

THIS profusely stepped specimen could have been inspired by a stack of railroad ties. As a climber anticipating your negotiation of the steps, you have the option of taking it in four steps or seven. It looks as if your ascent to the top would be easier in an approach from the left. However, until you actually try it, you cannot know for sure. The laws of energy conservation and expenditure may not apply in this uncanny world of the impossible!

The illusion has been accomplished by taking advantage of its equally spaced parallel lines in treating the end detail of the sticks, some of which seem to twist in order to comply with the illusion.

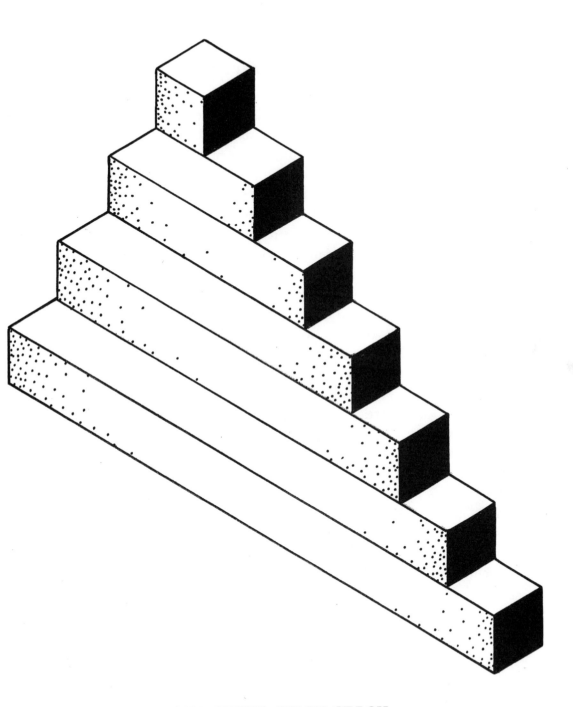

FOUR-SEVEN STICK STACK

Zip-Step Vertigo

THIS figure, a cousin to the tribar as well as to the "Endless Staircase," could perhaps be the ultimate stairmaster—if you turned it on its side. You could place it in your living room or garage for use in your daily twenty-minute aerobic exercise—sideways or upright! This wonder unit of meta-science could provide any desired incline from zero to 30 degrees without requiring an adjustment. Since there are no moving parts (except yourself!), it would never wear out. The only prerequisite might be a high ceiling, and the only problems that you might experience would be uncanny recurrent attacks of vertigo and déjà vu!

Upon close inspection you'll see that the "Zip-Step Vertigo" is made up of two subtly interconnected tribars, one placed above the other. The continuity of the walkway seems unbroken—until you realize that you can't decide on the status of the ambiguous vertical shaft, which extends straight up from the front of the pathway, ending behind it at the top. Both the far and near extremities of the seemingly level pathway are thus impossibly connected by the same vertical shaft, when in reality there should be two shafts. Thus, if you start walking at the bottom and travel the zigzag path, you will reach the top of the shaft. If the shaft were a hollow chute, you would drop straight down, right back to where you started. It is this same effect that made Escher's "Waterfall" work so well. The "Crazy Crate," discussed later, exhibits a similar discontinuity, where you are faced with a strategic vertical element that exists both in the background and the foreground. You can avoid the conflict only if you are able to mentally block out the vertical element.

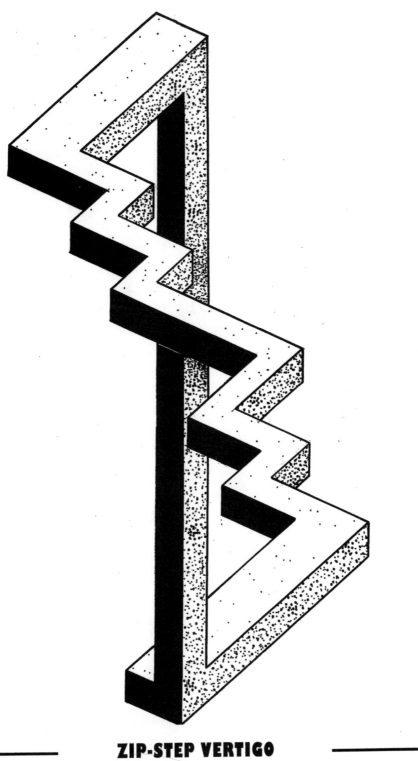

ZIP-STEP VERTIGO

Ambiguous Stepped Pyramid

THE figure on the facing page borrows from two classic impossible forms, the "Endless Staircase" and the "Space Fork." In this case, you have a choice: you may take the route on the right side and climb five full steps to get to the top, or, simply take one step onto the platform at the left, which will lead you ethereally to the top!

In the "Ambiguous Stepped Pyramid" each of the horizontal shafts between the voids at the left of the figure leads to a step on the right end, each at a different level. Also noteworthy is the fact that the opposite ends of the figure are not the same length, yet the number and size of tread elements are equal at both ends. The nagging question is, Are there five steps or just one?

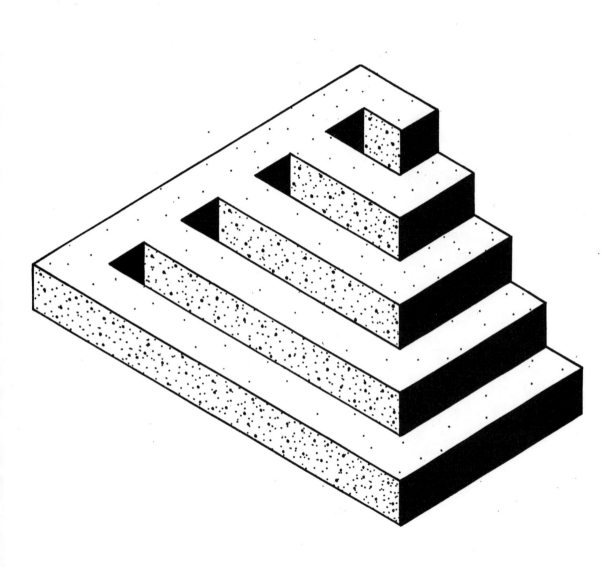

AMBIGUOUS STEPPED PYRAMID

Incongruous Stepped Wall

WITH this intriguing new figure, another impossible object is making its debut in this book. It combines subtle elements from both the "Endless Staircase" and the "Space Fork." These influences become evident, one way or another, when you examine the figure closely.

You will see that the figure is tied together by a single profound discontinuity: the front surface of the lower step "twists" toward the right and becomes a "floor" at the base of the wall. At the same time this effect causes us to confuse the opening in the wall with the shaded face of the second step.

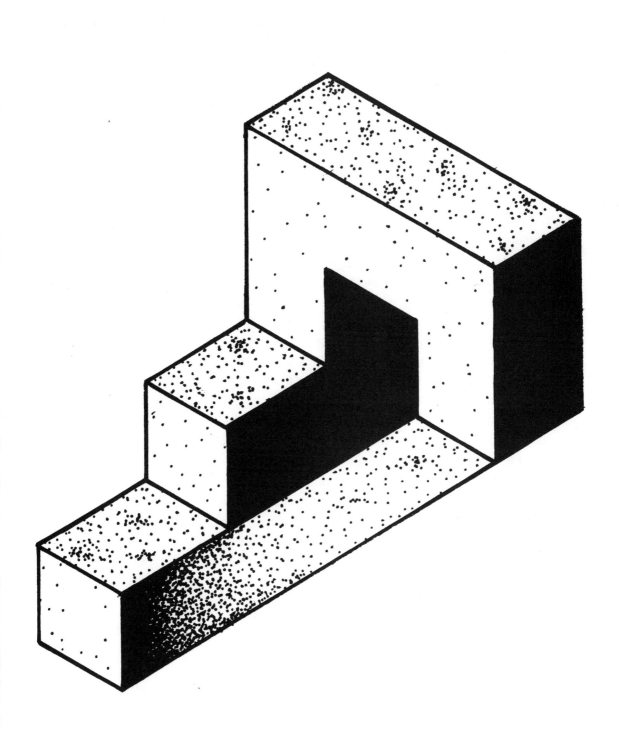

INCONGRUOUS STEPPED WALL

PART III

The Space Fork

WITH the "Space Fork," we enter the very heart and essence of Impossibilia. It represents what is probably the largest distinct family of impossible objects. Almost everyone has seen it at one time or other. It was this object that appeared one day on Mr. Thomas's bulletin board in the author's high school woodshop class, labeled simply "Space Fork." Even though I was unsuccessful in building such an object, I still got an "A" in Thomas's class, not to mention the fact that his pin-up triggered my interest in impossible objects, which led to a lifelong pursuit.

The notorious three-(or is it two-?) pronged impossible object as shown on page 51 began circulating among engineers and others in 1964. It first appeared in print as part of an advertisement by California Technical Industries in the March 23, 1964 issue of *Aviation Week and Space Technology* magazine. An article was published later that year by a psychology professor at Iowa State University in Ames, Iowa. It appeared in the December 1964 issue of the *American Journal of Psychology*. This was the first published writing about this ambiguous figure, which the author, Dr. Donald H. Schuster, called a "three-stick clevis." An actual shift in visual fixation is involved in perceiving and resolving (if that were possible) the incongruity in this new type of ambiguous figure. After much attention, scrutiny, and creative variations made by others over the years, Schuster's "Space Fork," has become a classic. A visually ambiguous trident or clevis-like device, of absolutely no practical use, it has also been called by some, simply, a "blivet." One rep from an aerospace manufacturer has suggested that its attributes be investigated for the design of an interdimensional cosmic tuning fork!

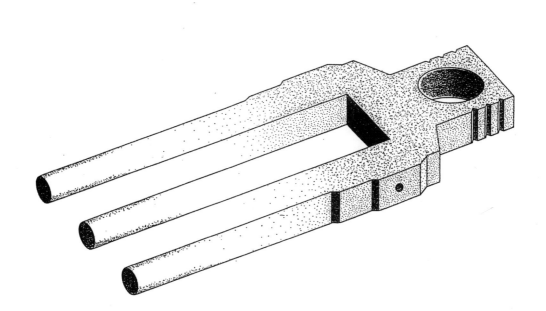

THE SPACE FORK

The Space Fork

I F you don't immediately perceive the impossibility of the object, it's probably due to the oscillation in your attention between the left and right sides
of the figure. Each of them separately is possible as a two-dimensional representation of the same solid object, but not when viewed together from the
same point in space.

The problem arises from an ambiguity in depth perception. Your eye is
not given the essential information necessary to locate the parts, and your
brain cannot make up its mind about what it's looking at. Your problem is to
determine the status of the middle prong. If you look at the left of the figure,
the three prongs all appear to be on the same plane; in other words, they
seem to share the same spatial-depth relationship. Yet, when you gaze at the
right of the figure, the middle prong appears to drop to a plane lower than
that of the two outer prongs. So just exactly where is the middle prong
located? It obviously cannot exist in both places at once. The confusion is a
direct result of your attempt to interpret the drawing as a three-dimensional
object.

The "Space Fork" works on the principle of the false connection—a
connection that can be made on a two-dimensional plane or surface, but not
in the three-dimensional world. The figure makes use of the fact that a
prong, round in cross section, can be represented by a pair of parallel lines,
while a beam, square in cross section, requires three lines. The illusion is
constructed by completing each pair of lines to make a prong at one end,
and each triad of lines to make a beam at the other end. The parallel lines
are equally spaced to emphasize the contradiction. If you could make a
cross-sectional "bread slice" cut through the middle of the "Space Fork,"
what do you think it would look like?

The figures shown on the following page represent two variations on the
"Space Fork."

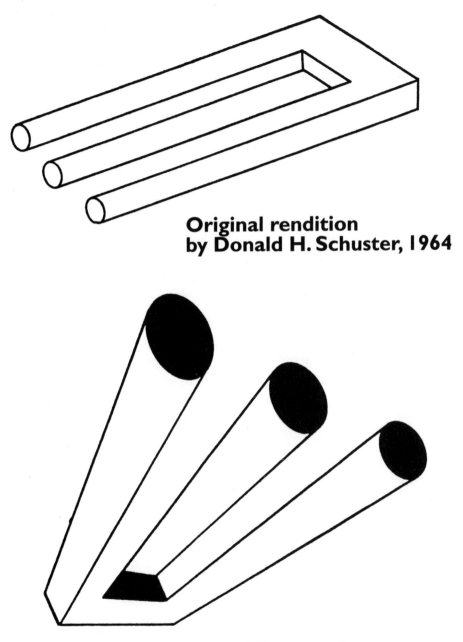

**Original rendition
by Donald H. Schuster, 1964**

Exaggerated Perspective

THE SPACE FORK

Ridge-Slotted Brick

THE object on the facing page is a technical variation of the "Space Fork" illusion. As you can see, it clearly applies the principle of the "Space Fork," but while the "Space Fork" is free floating, the "Ridge-Slotted Brick" is a floor-mounted fixture. In fact, if a metallurgist could be talked into fabricating such a thing out of iron, it might make a terrific interdimensional doorstop! The shop drawings could easily be drafted onto vellum, from which actual blueprints could be made. Of course, dimensioning the fluted top side might pose a problem, if the draftsman were to pay too close attention.

Like the famous "Space Fork," the "Ridge-Slotted Brick" functions on depth ambiguity. Convex edges at one end become concave at the other, while three distinct elements at one end dissolve into two at the other. The only real difference is that the three-two relationship is reversed, the trunk end being made up of three elements instead of two, as in the "Space Fork." Your problem, as you soon find out, is to establish order out of the continually chaotic, fluted top surface of the object. The confusion is a direct result of your attempt to interpret the drawing by conventional means. While the "Space Fork" uses precise parallel lines to expedite its illusion, the "Ridge-Slotted Brick" works best with lines that are slightly off parallel.

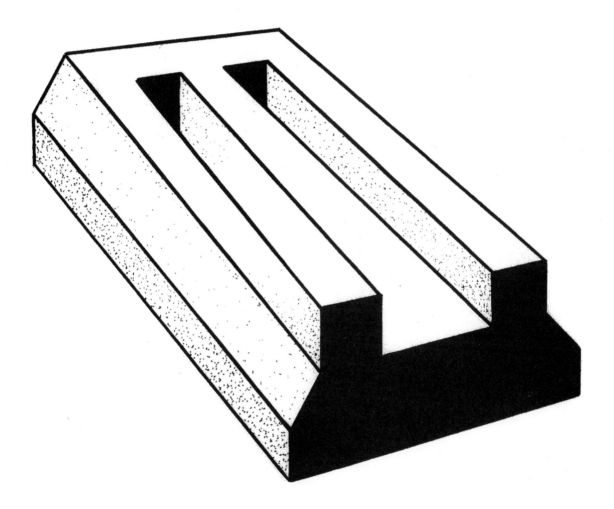

RIDGE-SLOTTED BRICK

Ridge-Slotted Block

THIS object, a third-generation technical variation on the "Space Fork" illusion, is similar to the last object. It is another in an almost endless stream of semi-interdimensional figures that can be developed on the principle of that classic.

Like the "Space Fork" and the "Ridge-Slotted Brick," the "Ridge-Slotted Block" shown here functions on an ambiguity in depth based on false connections between essentially parallel lines. Again, your problem, as you soon discover, is to establish order out of the visually induced oscillations in your gaze as you stare at the chaotic fluted surface of this object.

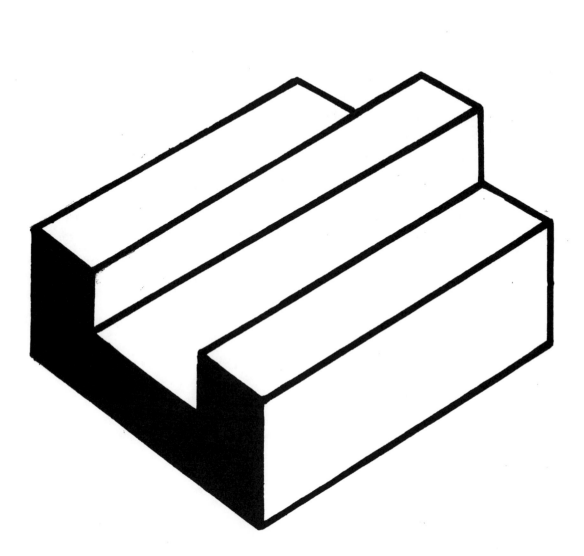

RIDGE-SLOTTED BLOCK

Outland Toaster

LIKE the other innovations just described, this figure is very much akin to the "Space Fork," as a number of elements on one end mysteriously gain a member at the other. Only, in this case, the whole figure is turned upright.

If you were to think of this device as a simple toaster in which to brown your daily bread, your experience might be an intriguing one. Imagine, for example, taking two slices of bread and placing them in the "Outland Toaster." What might happen when they pop up? Will there be two pieces of toast, or three? Whatever the outcome, this device might be as sought-after as the long-awaited free-energy device, or the mythical perpetual-motion machine!

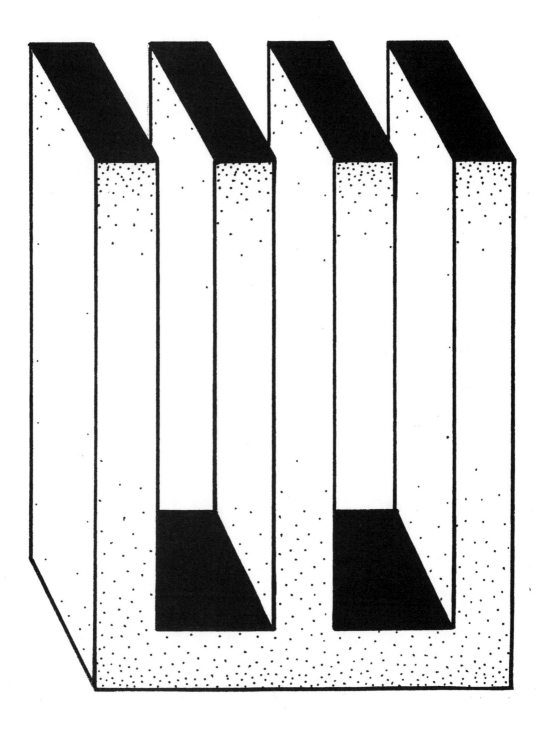

OUTLAND TOASTER

Twin-Columned Quadra-Tower

THE "Twin-Columned Quadra-Tower" exhibits, as its name implies, an obvious solid duality at its base. However, taking advantage of its parallel lines, the connections at the top produce an equally sound four-element crown piece. The visual ambiguity of this drawing overall is too great to resolve into a single solution. It is almost as difficult as imagining a square circle! This is another drawing where you can cover its lower two-thirds with your hand, and then move your hand down to amaze your friends with the big surprise at the bottom!

Like the "Outland Toaster," the curious object exhibited on the following page seems to hang on the "outland" of reality. Could it be a by-product of some bizarre government experiment? Or, could it be the schematic design for a midtown highrise? At any rate, this odd structure seems to have the uncanny ability to materialize or dematerialize at will. Then again, maybe it could be used as a new type of storage dump for the disposition of hazardous materials and substances!

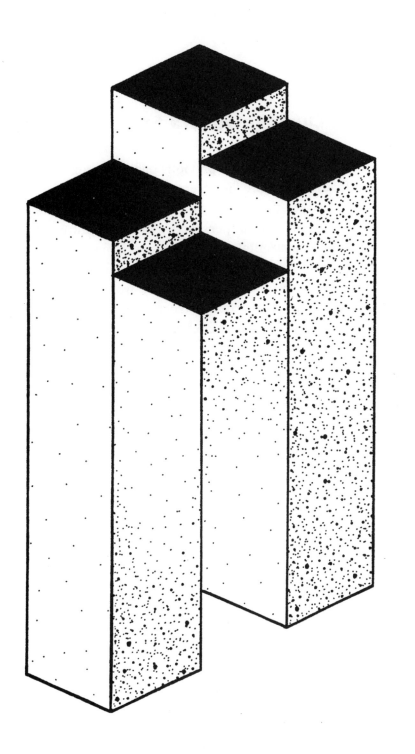

TWIN-COLUMNED QUADRA-TOWER

Dual Tri-Quadra Structure

As with the illusion shown on the previous page, the impossibility of the "Dual Tri-Quadra Structure" is accentuated by its strong vertical lines and texture. Here we see that the "magic" of impossible objects can be created not only from distortions in perspective or from contradictory visual cues, but from added horizontal or vertical textural peculiarities as well.

Another intriguing fact about this object is that is involves numeric indecision. Looking at the base, we see three pillars, from which we conclude that a total of four pillars supports the structure, assuming that one is located behind, hidden from view. Yet our assumption is not sound, for at the top we see that there are only three pillars, hence the name "Dual Tri-Quadra Structure"!

One interesting effect of impossible objects such as this is the sense of visual restlessness they seem to induce in the viewer. You will experience many "flavors" of the mind-eye experience as you progress through the illusions in this book. Among the unique visual attributes of impossible objects is their ability to perpetually defy integration. By the same token, they perpetually defy segregation!

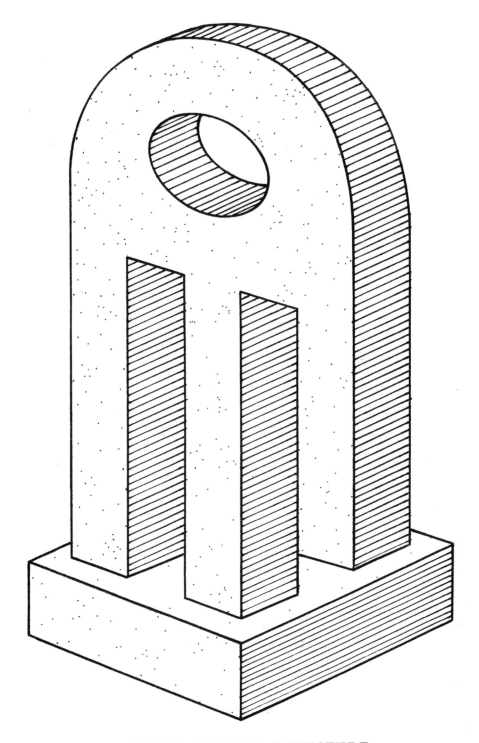

DUAL TRI-QUADRA STRUCTURE

Blivital Array

IN this figure we find a conjoining of what appears to be several space forks. By merging four space forks into a single vertical structure, and maintaining the all-important equal spacing between lines, we have produced an object that, from only four footings, springs forth with nine tines! As you recall, the original "Space Fork" produced three tines out of two shafts—but the "Blivital Array" more than doubles the original number of elements. Thus with a little experimentation we have produced the Blivet, or Space Fork, Extraordinaire! It might be possible to continue this experiment and create a mega-space fork by extending the base works infinitely—with the result being an endless array of upward-projecting tines!

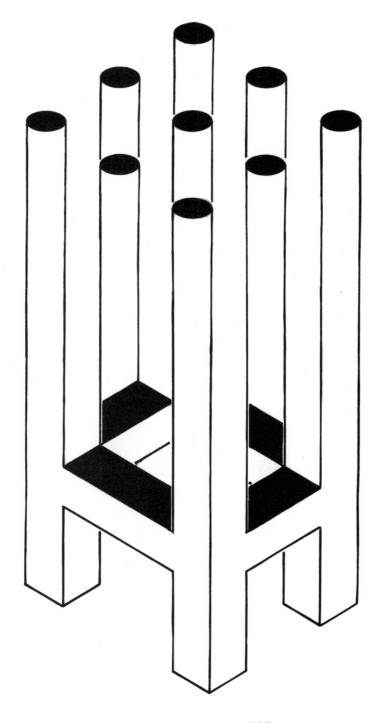

BLIVITAL ARRAY

Double Keys

BEFORE we move on to the next major segment in our tour of Impossibilia we must consider a strange subset of Fork-related, stick-style entities—bars that resemble piano keys. The principle of the "Double Keys," which incorporate this effect, actually is the same as that of the "Space Fork"—false connections that cause one or more elements to retreat to a different plane. As you first glance to the left of this figure, it seems to be composed of two ends with a wide gap between them. Yet, as you look to the right you see two ends in contact, which cast a strong shadow. Once you perceive the ambiguity of the figure, your gaze seems caught up in a visual back-and-forth that may continue for some time, as you try to count the bars. It's a lot like looking at the "Space Fork," but in a fresh new way. In this case, the number of elements at each end remains the same, but one component seems to materialize out of its neighbor, while another arises out of the shadows.

Existing at the outland of reality, this figure seems to represent a prime example of both a material and nonmaterial object! In this case the shadow, which becomes part of the solid element in the foreground, reinforces the ambiguity, and an element at the right vanishes into nothingness, becoming a void at the left. It is the shadow along with false connections that creates this unique and innovative new illusion. Of course, none of this would be possible in the real world, yet here it is, the unimaginable, right before your very eyes!

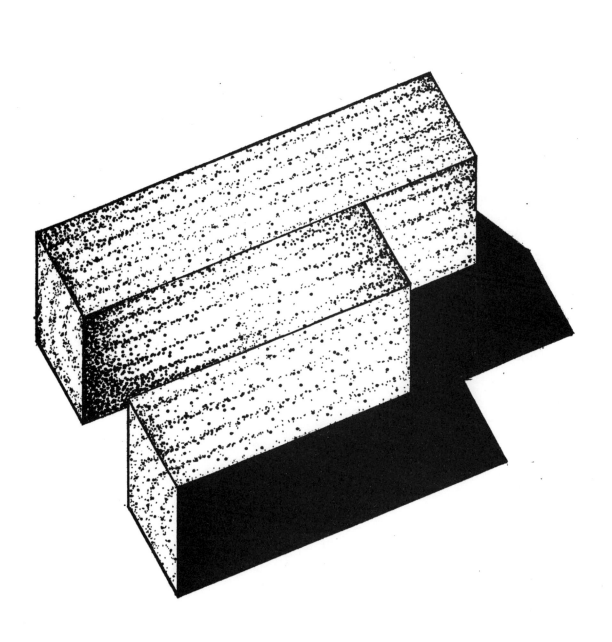

DOUBLE KEYS

Tri-Quadra Bar

THE "Tri-Quadra Bar" is a stick-style impossible object that also operates on the same principle as the "Space Fork." In this case, there are not just two bars that dissolve into three, but three bars that dissolve into four. The parallel relationships of equally spaced lines are fundamental to the success of this illusion. A gaze at the right extremity, followed by a visual sweep toward the left, seems to cause your stare to split, as one element of the illusion becomes part of two others.

Where does reality end and impossibility begin? Many of these objects leave it up to the hardworking eye to figure that out. Our day-to-day experiences with external objects make it very difficult to accept concepts that we cannot understand intuitively. Thus, through our encounters with impossible figures, we recognize that perception is a continuous series of simple hypotheses about the external world, built up through sensory experience. (And it doesn't even take a psychologist to tell you that!)

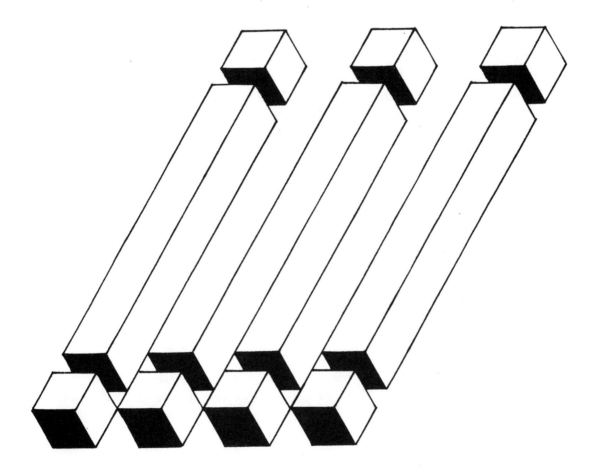

TRI-QUADRA BAR

Dual-End Bi-Post

SIMPLICITY is a virtue of profundity, for the former is what often makes for the latter. When something is clear, concise, and simple, it is often said to be brave, bold, and relevant! Now, the "Dual-End Bi-Post" may not be any of the aforementioned, because it is a contradiction, and quite impossible!

Visual communication is a universal language. It has no limits of tongue, vocabulary, or grammar, and can be perceived by the illiterate as well as the literate. Visual imagery can often convey facts and ideas in a deeper, wider, and more articulate manner than almost any other means of communication. It can reiterate and reinforce verbal concepts with such sensory richness that no one would want to add even a word! Yet (and we must drop a bomb on what has just been said) impossible objects do just the opposite: they contaminate and confuse visual communication. If we tried to verbally describe an impossible object to someone—over the telephone, for instance—the person at the other end of the line would not likely be able to draw it. Then the question might be raised: Of what use is this strange new-fangled device?

The "Dual-End Bi-Post" might, after all, have a most practical application. It could prove most valuable as a dual-purpose bi-post for shoring up a mine shaft. If the mine were to collapse, the bi-post could suddenly become two posts, thereby reinforcing the shaft and preventing the collapse in the first place!

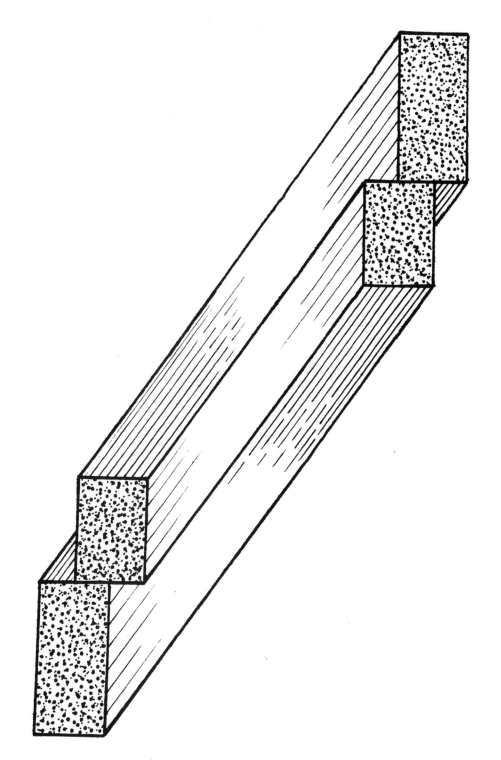

DUAL-END BI-POST

PART IV

The Crazy Crate

A new impossible object made its debut in 1966 as a result of the experiments of Dr. Charles F. Cochran, a photographer, in Chicago, Illinois. Cochran's "trick" photograph of his "Crazy Crate" appeared in the June 1966 issue of *Scientific American* magazine. Many impossiblers have since experimented with the "Crazy Crate," and now the figure stands as one of the classic "Big Four," a status shared with the "Impossible Triangle," the "Endless Staircase" and the "Space Fork." Its originator first called it the "Freemish Crate," and claimed it was "built for the shipment of optical illusions in quantity." Others have added that this impossible box is just great for carrying widgets and other unidentifiable objects.

The impossible crate is an ambiguous inside-out skeletal cube that causes a visual-mental shock when you see it, a result of the fluctuation between two opposing perceptual interpretations. A coherent solution never emerges. As in so many impossible objects, the "Crazy Crate" works through false connections in the drawing.

The immediate predecessor of the "Crazy Crate" was the "impossible box" held by a seated lad in M.C. Escher's famous 1958 etching, "Belvedere." Escher's impossible box, in turn, had its origins in the Necker Cube, which is not an impossible object but an ambiguous figure involving depth reversal.

The Necker Cube was first described in 1832 by the Swiss crystallographer Louis A. Necker, who noticed that crystals sometimes appeared to change in shape as he looked at them. The Necker Cube can be seen as a two-dimensional flat surface, but due to the way we look at things, it is actually more difficult for us to see it in two dimensions than in three. When we stare at the Necker Cube, we experience a figure alternating in depth—sometimes one face lies in the front, then the same face lies in the back. It jumps suddenly from one position to the other. Our perception goes on a dynamic search for the best interpretation of the available data. How much our past experience and learning affect our interpretation is a mystery. This factor is significant, though, in the creation of impossible objects that, like the Necker Cube, "jam" our perceptive processes.

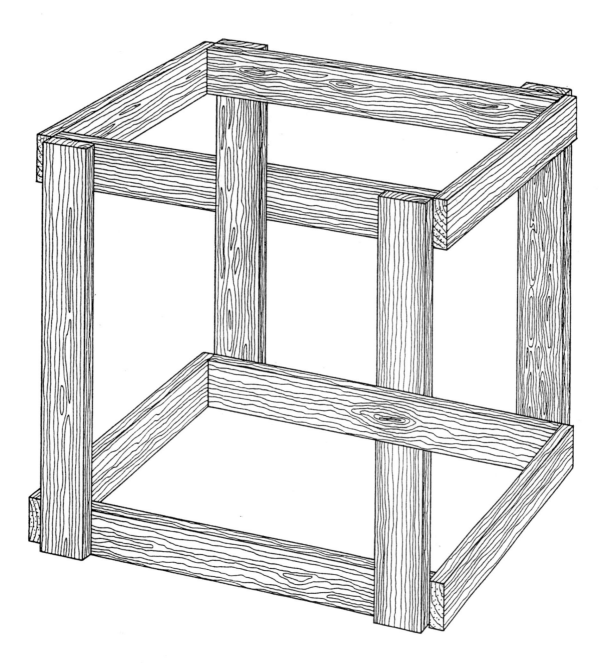

THE CRAZY CRATE

The sequence of illustrations that follow shows how the skeletal cube developed in relation to impossible objects. The image on the top shows the original Necker Cube. (Notice how the little black ball sometimes appears in the cube's front face, and sometimes in the back face, and in the corner, or center). The image to the right shows how Escher applied Necker's Cube. The image below, in turn, shows Dr. Cochran's rendition of Escher's Impossible Cube. There have been many variations of the cube in its application to impossible objects as others have experimented with its possibilities.

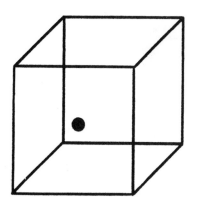

Necker's Cube

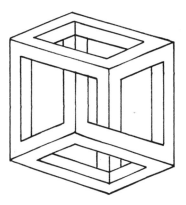

Escher's Cube

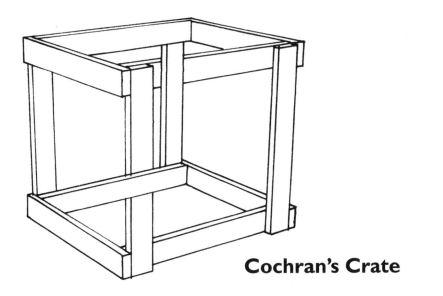

Cochran's Crate

An ambiguous figure is one that you can interpret in two or more ways, as in the case of the Necker Cube, which exhibits depth reversal. It is drawn without perspective or any size difference that would give us a clue as to which part of it is closer or further away. Yet we still see in the Necker Cube a three dimensionality that demands a concrete solution. Ambiguity is, of course, the hallmark of all impossible objects, which have also been called "ambiguous figures." However, impossible objects go a step beyond mere ambiguity. Through their wild fluctuations between two sharply contrasting solutions they continually defy the eye as it vainly roves around the figure, until the mind eventually concedes that they are indeed impossible.

The Necker Cube has been the fountainhead of all cubular impossible objects. Yet it is not the only ambiguous figure involving depth reversal, and not the only one that has been involved in the creation of impossible objects. Other ambiguous figures include Mach's "Reversible Book" and Schröder's "Staircase." These figures, however, are not to be confused with those that involve a figure-ground reversal. In a figure-ground reversal your eye moves spontaneously, alternating between the figure and the background as they seem to compete for dominance. Probably the best example is Rubin's "Vase-Profile Figure," which has appeared in print in countless versions. The principle of figure-ground reversal has also been useful in the creation of impossible objects. "Double Keys" (page 64), with its strong shadows, is an example of this, at least in part.

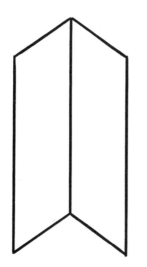

Mach's Reversible Book

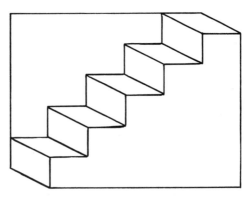

Schröder's Staircase

Rubin's Vase-Profile

Integral Cube

As stated earlier, the "Crazy Crate" developed from the impossible cube held by the youth in M.C. Escher's "Belvedere," which in turn was inspired by L.A. Necker's Cube. As before, one man builds upon the work of another—one man discovers or invents, a second man improvises, and a third man develops and improves! In like fashion, we now have a fourth-generation impossible cube, the "Integral Cube"—just one result of many more recent experiments with cubes. The cube is an amazingly flexible figure, capable of producing a wide range of variations. It can be modified a great deal without losing its overall identity as a cube. The example shown here, as in so many cases, functions through a depth ambiguity based on false connections.

The "Integral Cube" makes use of strange corner connections, connections that are not created in the manner we would normally expect. Front corners are not always connected to other front corners, but to side points and rear extremities. For instance, one vertical part is connected at its top end to a horizontal part that seems at first to be the top front of the cube, but then appears to be the bottom of the back side of the cube. In addition to peculiar corner connections, this figure incorporates odd shadings and other unexpected coverings and joinings.

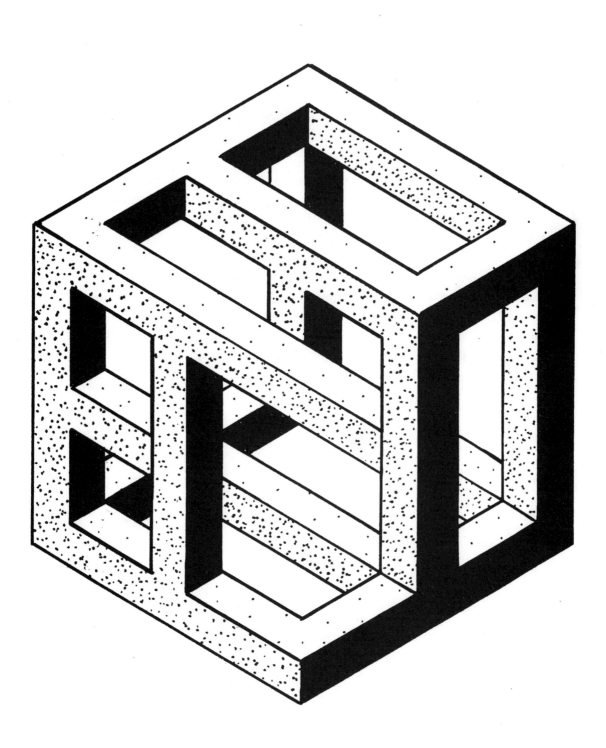

INTEGRAL CUBE

Escalating Cube

WHILE ambiguous depth-reversal figures throw the mind into a state of indecision, impossible cubes take us a step further into befuddlement. The concept of the impossible cube has now been telescoped into the intriguing figure dubbed the "Escalating Cube," which has expanding or reducing possibilities.

In this figure downsized cubes are developed into one entity. A thin wall on the left and a massive wall on the right share a common plane at the left and bottom, but not at the right and top. Tucked between them are ever-smaller cubes that demonstrate the same properties. The process of using still smaller cubes, or larger for that matter, could go on forever. Another name for this object, therefore, could be the "Infinity Cube."

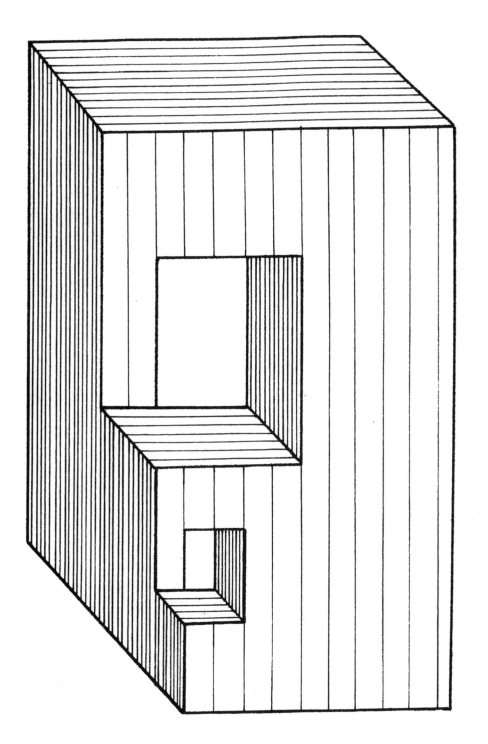

ESCALATING CUBE

Integral Cubicle

THE "Integral Cubicle" shown on the facing page is another variation on the cube theme. At first glance, you seem to see two distinct clusters of cubes as if they were fused together. Then, on second glance, a curious discontinuity becomes evident. The right-side face of one set of cubes suddenly becomes the left-side face of the other set of cubes. As with Necker's Cube, your mind cannot decide which concept to adopt.

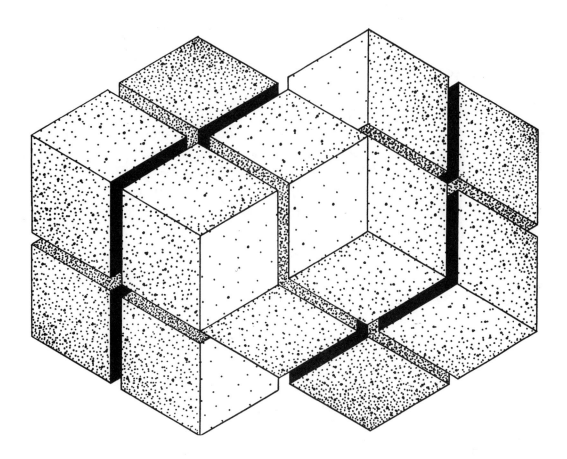

INTEGRAL CUBICLE

Pavilion of Cubes

HERE we see the standard cube-block unit in another unique construction, this time in an architectural treatment. Inspired by a set of children's building blocks, we have constructed a complex edifice employing a number of cleverly misplaced elements in perspective, somewhat reminiscent of the Integral Cube on page 76. In this instance we have a system of structural bearing points and "roof" lines that do not conform to the "footprint" of the floor and foundation plan. The "Pavilion of Cubes" is another example of the infinite number of applications of impossibilic technology that can be encouraged in the building industry!

PAVILION OF CUBES

Cubes in Repetition

IN the illustration on the next page, you are presented with a figure that
seems to exist in a single plane. After you glance at the figure for just a
fleeting moment, however, you become aware that it extends out at a right
angle as well, while still maintaining its apparent overall single-plane orientation. Since this figure partially incorporates the principle of the triangle, it
could have been classified with the tribar. However, while the triangle represents three angles, the cube represents three dimensions, so we have
grouped this figure with the cube-style impossible objects.

The children's pastime of arranging blocks seems to be a favorite activity
among creators of impossible objects. In this array, each block appears to be
a "toy" that can be played with and put into an assemblage with other
blocks. If toy manufacturers could mass-produce individual units of the
"Cubes in Repetition" on an assembly line, they would likely be top sellers
at the retail level!

CUBES IN REPETITION

Cubular Snowflake

IN this figure we again see an impossible object that functions like the "Crazy Crate" or Escher's Impossible Box. Unlike many of the impossible figures that work on false connections and oscillating planes in perspective, the Cubular Snowflake holds together by means of a false orientation. The core element suddenly becomes tied to the outer arrangement. As in the Necker Cube, this figure seems to oscillate between concave and convex configurations.

In another sense, you could consider this figure an illustration of depth reversal, as borrowed from the Necker Cube. As we see in this example and others like it, this principle can be put to great effect in the creation of impossible worlds.

CUBULAR SNOWFLAKE

Indented Sand Blocks

THIS figure functions primarily on depth-projection ambiguity. One element seems obviously in front of the other, but when you consider another portion of the element, it appears to be behind its companion piece. Meanwhile, its counterpart demonstrates the same effect. That's why we have classified it with the cube—it has one or more portions "tucked under." At the same time, at work in the figure are false connections in perspective. You might say that this figure functions on three levels. It is another impossible variation made possible by the principles of the "Crazy Crate."

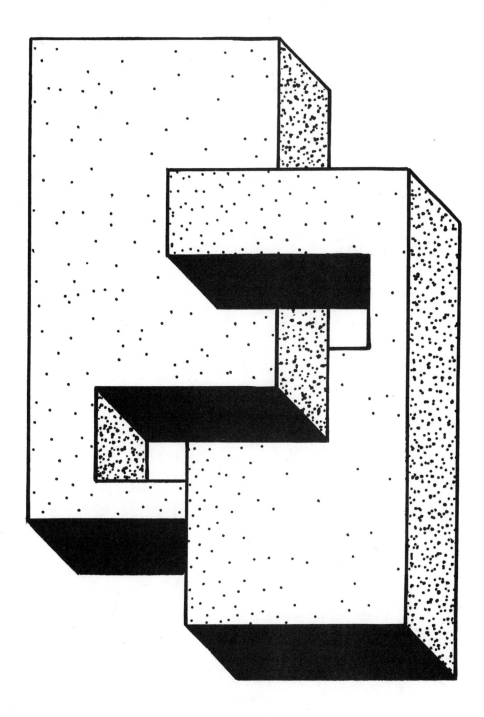

INDENTED SAND BLOCKS

Cubes in Limbo

THE figure on the next page seems to be, at first glance, an acceptable arrangement of cubes. But, after a closer look you realize that there is something decidedly wrong. If you count the cubes they add up to four, yet the cube at the lower right is both a rear cube and a front cube at the same time. Check it out.

CUBES IN LIMBO

Two-Story Cube

THE object featured on the next page is another innovative variation of the basic impossible cube. In this figure we see what appears to be, at first glance, a structure consisting of four vertical members with cross members at mid-height. But it does not take long to see that there is something very unusual about this object. The cross members at mid-height are connected to the structure in an impossible way. They extend from the left and right verticals back to a rear vertical, which is, in reality, the front vertical—if you look at the top and bottom. In this figure we encounter a circumstance similar to that found in the "Space Fork"—confusion about the status of the middle member. If it is either the front or rear vertical, then where is the fourth vertical support? According to our view through the window at the top, there is no rear vertical. Yet, what we see at mid-height tells us that there has to be a rear vertical. The odd horizontals of this "two-story" cube seem to turn it wrong-side out—without bending it or deforming it—not even one inch!

TWO-STORY CUBE

Multifaceted Cinder Block

THIS strange new figure is yet another startling variation on the impossible cube. This time we see what at first seems a decorative concrete block for building construction or landscaping. As we look closer, however, our attention is caught by the details in its center cavity, which are oriented in an impossible manner.

We are looking at an example of planar discontinuity. This occurs where an element in the drawing appears in more than one pictorial plane. For example, the middle left-right element in the cavity exists in at least three different planes—in the face of the block, in the plane of the single top-to-bottom element in the cavity under which it dips, and then in its own position beneath the cross bars. Meanwhile, the top-to-bottom element in the cavity passes effortlessly from top to bottom, alternately dipping and rising as it weaves between the horizontals, yet it is not bent at all and shows no sign of trauma.

The two primary indicators of what's wrong in this drawing are the outside of the front, which continually tells us that the face is flat, and the center vertical element, which blatantly passes behind, and then in front, of its companions. From an architectural standpoint, a schematic like this could serve as a plan for a four-story apartment house without any need for a stairway or an elevator! This figure may also remind you of a type of construction project—a tunnel, for instance—where teams of workers start at opposite ends and dig toward a meeting point at the center, where they inevitably miss each other. Except, in this case, they don't miss!

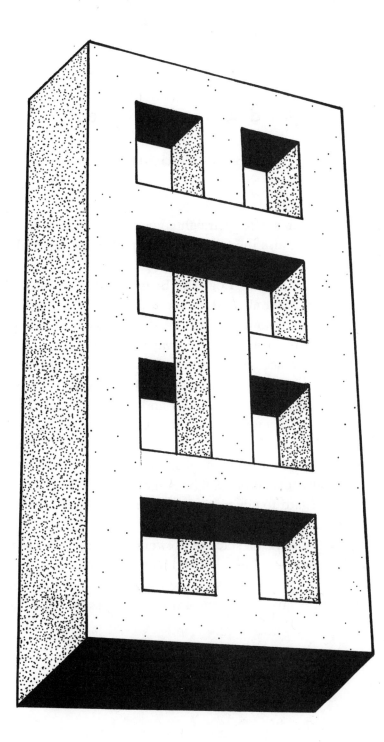

MULTIFACETED CINDER BLOCK

PART V

Hybrid Impossible Objects

Logs and Beams

HERE we open up a whole new realm of hybrid impossibilities. Up to this point the draftsman's board, straightedge, and triangle have been used to create figures. Now we use the Circle and Ellipse templates, and the French curve (see page 7).

In this unique new figure, "Logs and Beams," three beams seem to quite normally touch each other along their common edges. But, at their right angle a startling new phenomenon occurs: three massive cylinders, almost as if forced through, easily "squeeze" their way between the beams. Yet, the three beams have no space between them. How can this be? Is this a dream come true, in principle, for a new building technology that allows a person to enter a building through a closed door and go out through a wall? Perhaps it could offer an easy way to stack logs between railroad ties in a storage yard!

This figure works in a manner similar to the "Space Fork," in that it makes use of equally spaced parallel lines. The logs are simply drawn into the rails, without regard to any rule of perspective. In fact, anything you wanted could be drawn between the rails.

If this thing(s) were just a stack of firewood waiting to be ignited by a match, you might wonder about which direction the flames would burn, especially around the area of the supposed space between the beams. Indeed, "Logs and Beams" has some amazing impossibilities!

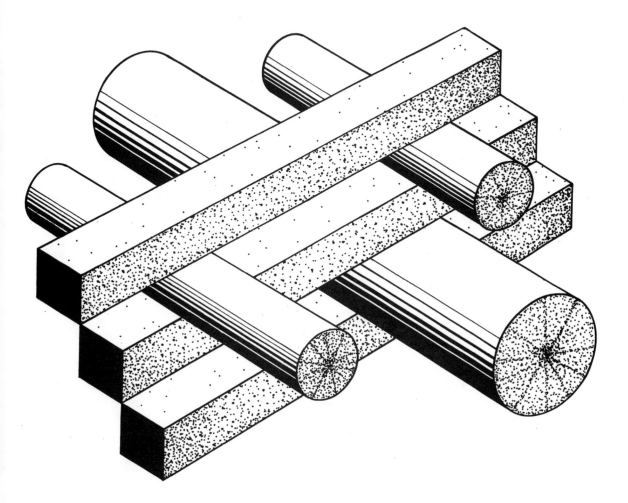

LOGS AND BEAMS

Incongruous Barbell

IN another circular impossibility we might ask: How can a straight bar wrap itself around another object without bending? The "Incongruous Barbell" is a device that seems to do just that. As you can see, the left disk or weight is drawn in a way that gives the illusion of a traversing rod that is neither bent or straight.

The "Incongruous Barbell" leaves you wondering what effect this device would have, as an exercise piece, upon the development of your biceps and triceps. The next time you go to the gym to use this piece of equipment in a workout, make sure the safety collars on your weights are secured and, by all means, check the orientation of the disks. Otherwise, it may be impossible to grip the object!

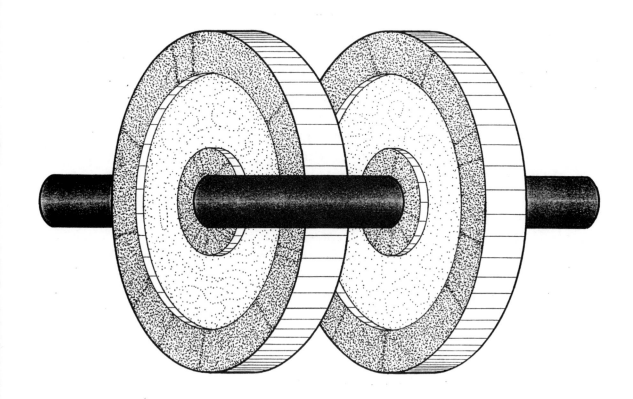

INCONGRUOUS BARBELL

Impossible Paper Clip

WHERE is the impossibility in this drawing? Certainly not in the realm of the two-dimensional. It looks simple enough, until you realize its contradictory visual cues. This figure makes use of an important principle of impossibiliting—the misplaced delineation, a device often used in this book. For instance, the left-hand side of the vertical element contacts the horizontal element in the background—not the foreground, as reality would demand. Likewise, the horizontal element is turned ninety degrees counterclockwise from where it ought to be. However, if we stuck with these rules, the vertical paper-clip-like element that we see here would not fit neatly onto, or into and through, the horizontal popsicle-stick-like element in such a fascinating way!

The "Impossible Paper Clip" represented here is supposedly made from wood, although paper clips are usually made of metal. Actually, though, it is uncertain what this object is made of—if it is made at all! But we find it difficult to view this figure in two dimensions, because our world is so much more than that.

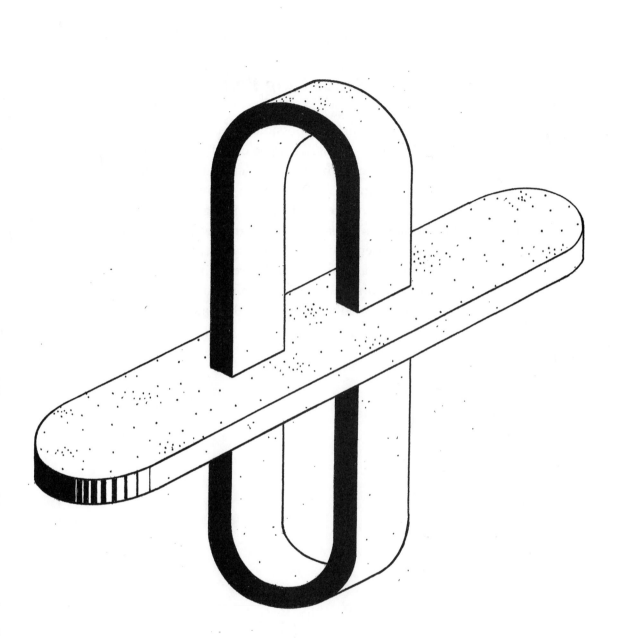

IMPOSSIBLE PAPER CLIP

Ambiguous Ring Illusion

INALLY, we round out our tour of impossible objects with this figure—the "Ambiguous Ring Illusion." It might also be called the "Dual Ellipse," the "Ambiguous Ellipse," or even the "Contradictory Dual Oval," because it neatly fits all these descriptions. Whatever you wish to call it, it is truly a marvel of technical graphics and certainly a very intriguing visual paradox.

The "Ambiguous Ring" is consistent in its extremities but, as is often the case with these figures, nonsensical overall. You can demonstrate this by covering the left-hand or right-hand half of the figure with a sheet of paper. The visible portion will appear correct, but when you remove the paper, the figure's ambiguity becomes decidedly apparent, to the point of incredibility!

AMBIGUOUS RING ILLUSION

PART VI

You Can Make an Impossible Object

AN impossible object is actually not difficult to create. With some study of common geometric shapes, coupled with a bit of imagination, you can do it in minutes. The profound arrangement of cubes shown on the facing page was created in less than five minutes after staring at the checkerboard pattern of squares in a linoleum tile floor. After a preliminary sketch of the tile floor pattern was made, a dimension of depth was added. Then after a bit of "playing" with the figure, this unique configuration was born. Because the method of creating impossible objects follows rather narrow graphic constraints, it should come as no surprise that two people working independently might come up with a common or similar product.

The inspiration for a drawing of an impossible object may come from any one of a number of sources. The figures in this book were inspired by common everyday household items, and a few other more or less domestic items. Then, with a touch of imagination, they were reinterpreted, translated, and developed into their fullest expression. Finding potential impossible objects as such can be as exciting as a treasure hunt. It is a challenge to see how many you can find or come up with in simple sketches. Then you can give them your own names, which is even more fun!

Perhaps the best way to get started is to take sketch pad and pencil in hand and begin by sketching copies of familiar everyday objects. Don't take on anything too complicated; stick with objects of simple geometric form. Once you've sketched something, start playing around with your idea, experimenting with it in successive drawings. It might take a little practice, but you'll be amazed at what you end up with. Your assignment, should you choose to accept it, is to create your own homemade impossible object!

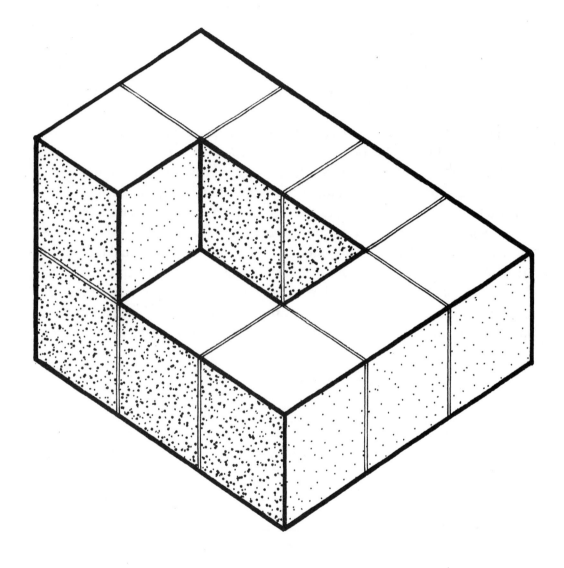

A HOMEMADE IMPOSSIBLE OBJECT

Space Frame

THIS figure was inspired by a doorway. Is it real, unreal, maybe surreal? Is it a door leading to the infinite, or a schematic design for a new kind of box frame for a bed? If the latter, perhaps such an outlandish bed might be useful in reducing sleeplessness!

In the "Space Frame" the visual ambiguity is similar to that used in many other figures in this book—false connections in perspective. If you look at one end of the figure, the bottom end for instance, you will realize that you are seeing it from a point above rather than below it, which is not consistent with the perspective of the top. In other words, we have a bird's-eye view and a worm's-eye view of the figure at the same time, which in reality is impossible. This effect has been accomplished simply by making both ends of the figure identical. This was easy enough because the three parallel lines of the long axis elements were equally spaced, making it easy to create the false connections at the ends. The unreal "Space Frame," and an inset showing how the true perspective should actually look in reality, appear on the next page.

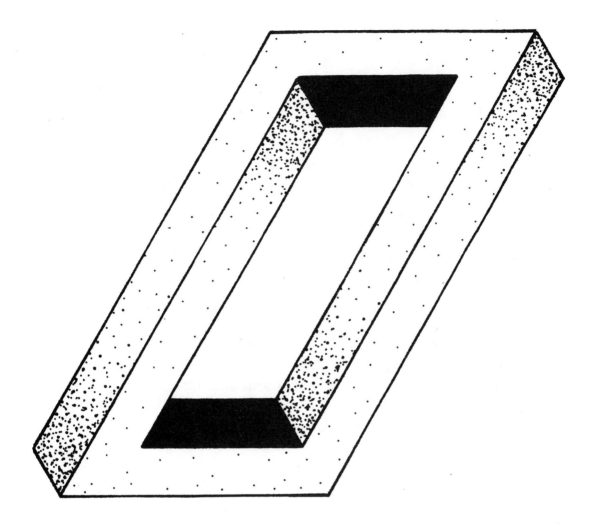

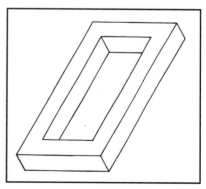

SPACE FRAME

Double Space Frame

To create this drawing we simply took the doorway theme of the last figure one step further. This illusion has three parallel vertical elements, all apparently on the same plane, and a top and bottom that appear to cross each other perpendicularly and in duplicate. What appears at the top is not so at the bottom, and what appears at the bottom is not so at the top. Using misplaced connections in perspective by taking advantage of equally spaced parallel lines, as before we get both a bird's-eye and a worm's-eye view at the same time. The "Double Space Frame" consists of the elements of a perfectly normal frame as seen from two different directions and, as a whole, it seems to be an intact spatial structure.

While this object may seem to resemble a warped double window frame, the similarity is only apparent. You can be sure that officials at the building trades commission would be at a loss to find an entry for it in their product listings! Then again, and just perhaps, it may be that alleged window to infinity. Could there be such a thing in the physical universe?

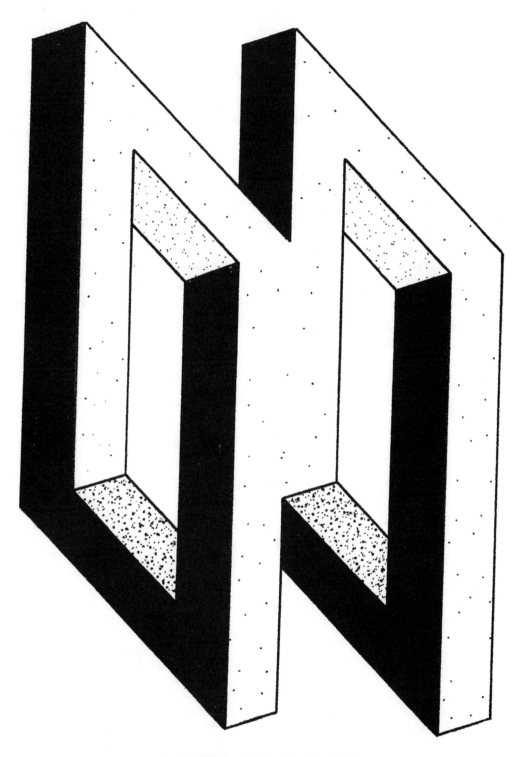

DOUBLE SPACE FRAME

Double Clevis

HERE is another unique innovation direct from the world of the impossible, the anomalous "Double Clevis." One of many figures developed from the tribar, it seems, at first glance, to exist in a single geometric plane, but then you realize that it exists in two planes at right angles to each other. Still, over-all, you feel it is a one-plane figure.

You can create your own "Double Clevis," or any other double-whatever, by cleaving to the principles mentioned in this book and taking a good look at the myriad of inspirations that surround you in your everyday life. Then, just use your imagination. Oh, yes, don't forget to think of a sensible, or nonsensi-cal, name for your invention!

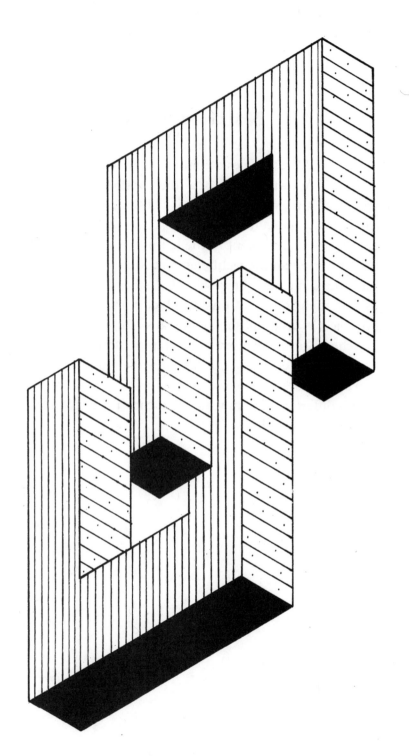

DOUBLE CLEVIS

Notched Brick

THE "Notched Brick" resembles a cube of butter or fudge with a bionic bite taken out of it. The vertical surface at the foreground appears as a single flat plane in perspective, yet when you look at the elements on either side of the cleavage more carefully, they seem to oscillate uncontrollably between two separate planes. The element to the left of the slot seems to hover in a position further back than the right element. Meanwhile, the top surface seems to show the same eerie behavior, also occupying two planes in perspective. As with many other impossible objects, the convincingly confusing effect of this object is accomplished by means of misplaced connections.

The "Notched Brick," inspired by a scrap of lumber at a construction site (or it could have been a brick) is a rectangular solid—one of the easiest geometric forms to work with in creating impossible objects. To examine and "play" with different ways in which you can "redesign" such a geometric solid, start by just drawing lines!

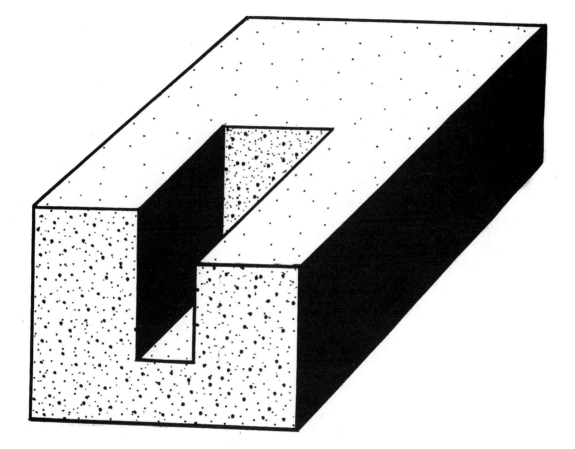

NOTCHED BRICK

Replicating Cube

IMPOSSIBLE cubes know no limit. Each new variety goes a step further than the last, throwing the mind into a further state of confused delight. Like its simpler predecessor, the "Escalating Cube" (page 78), the "Replicating Cube" has a row of expanding or reducing windows. In this figure, which resembles the starting gate at a race track, upsized cubes are developed into more expanded entities, which could conceivably be expanded forever.

In another sense, the "Replicating Cube" could be the inspiration for a unique architectural innovation. The sills of the four windows seem to be aligned in a straight row, but then, as you look at the top of the figure, it seems obvious that they are not. You could argue with yourself, "Yes, they are," "No, they're not," "Yes, they are," ad infinitum, and you'd both be right! As with the "Escalating Cube," this figure poses no limit to the ardent and imaginative cuboholic!

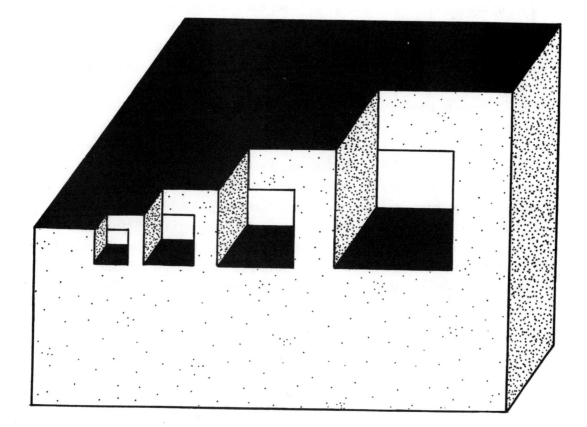

REPLICATING CUBE

Opposing Timbers

THE figure shown on the facing page uses the same bird's-eye/worm's-eye line connection technique as the "Dual-End Bi-Post" on page 68. As before, two opposing ends of the same entity project into the foreground, but in a unique new design. As before, even though in real life this figure would have to be bent 180 degrees in order to accomplish what we see, there appears to be no evidence of trauma or torsion in the material, no cracks, ripples, or any other production flaws!

What scientists, politicians, or journalists would not love to get their hands on one of these?! It would be a great toy for fidgeting with during lengthy strategy meetings or press conferences. Or, could it be used as a fantastic futuristic interdimensional combination stun gun and communications device for space travelers? The "Opposing Timbers" may indeed be one of those upcoming by-products of impossible research where funding is poured into a financial black hole. Wouldn't these little jewels sell like hotcakes at the next Trek convention? Why not begin now to invent your very own version of the "Opposing Timbers"? You might just really stun someone!

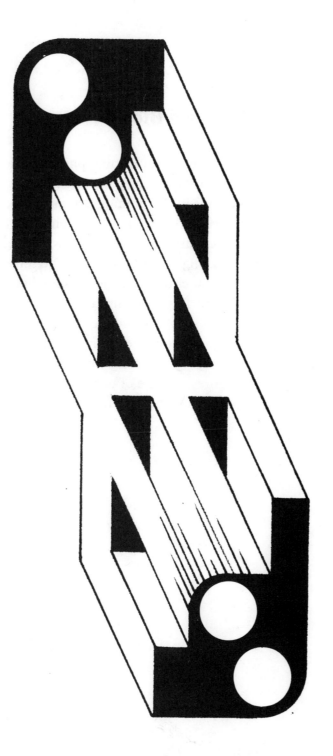

OPPOSING TIMBERS

Integral Block

As we have seen before, blocks make great inspirations for impossible objects. The object appearing on the facing page might have been derived from an arrangement of wood studs in the framing details of a new house. The first thing we probably notice in this figure is the dominant clean-cut, left-facing U-shaped element, then, an instant later, the well-integrated, upside-down reverse-J element facing toward the right. The sensation of depth in the figure is created almost entirely by the darkened surface at the bottom of the apparent slot. Yet this feature contradicts the correspondingly shaded top surface of the figure. It is as if the whole object has been twisted, or contorted, in order to make it stand on its own integrity. Yet, it has no integrity, because it seems to be saying one thing while doing another! Again, as in other impossible figures, the use of parallel lines and false connections in perspective have joined together in this truly impossible thing!

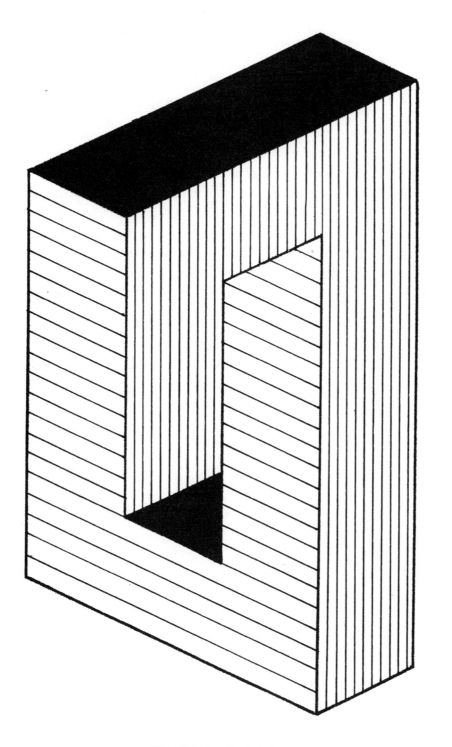

INTEGRAL BLOCK

Self-Embracing Block

IN a mixture of cubular and tribar elements, this object exists by virtue of a "twist" in perspective, in a similar technique to the one used in the "Space Frame," "Double Space Frame," and the "Opposing Timbers." In this case, it is as if your eyes have been widened so that they are further apart in order to see around both sides of the figure. Of course, through a trick of perspective, this amazing new power lies in the figure itself, not in you. It seems that the only power you feel, as you mentally embrace this figure, is the power to be confused! If you are interested in contesting that theory, try building a model!

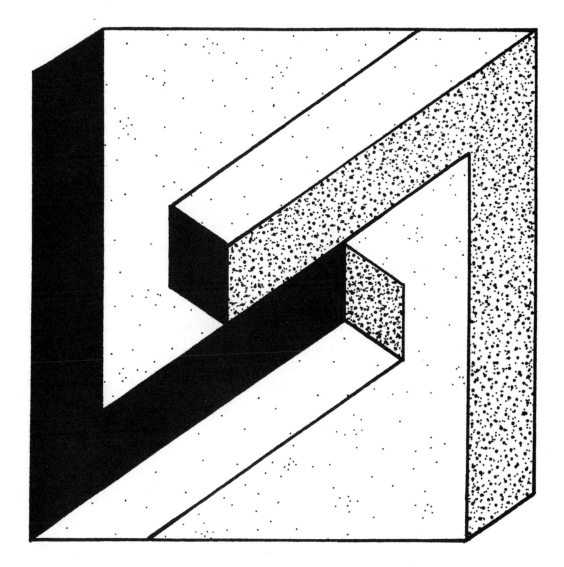

SELF-EMBRACING BLOCK

Stubbed Tribar

JUST now introduced into the world of Impossibilia, the figure exhibited on the facing page is yet another unique object never before published, at least to our knowledge! This figure represents a clear message on how easy it is to be innovative in the world of the impossible.

The "Stubbed Tribar" seems to be a cross between a cube and a tribar. However, what we have accomplished here is a simple "cut and repair" at the top corner, which results in a whole new image. The dominant left vertical shaft leads upward to the newly created level plane at the top. When you cross it, you are led, in a roundabout way, back "down" to the bottom at the base of the shaft where you started.

The inspiration for this figure is the "Impossible Triangle," but the "Stubbed Tribar" was not developed directly from the tribar but by using the same principle used to create the tribar. By playing around with the tribar concept, kicking it around, so to speak, and trying out various ways of connecting the lines, you will undoubtedly end up with something that works as an impossible object (you will know when that happens). Through such experiments it is possible to come up with many unique and innovative new objects that are decidedly impossible!

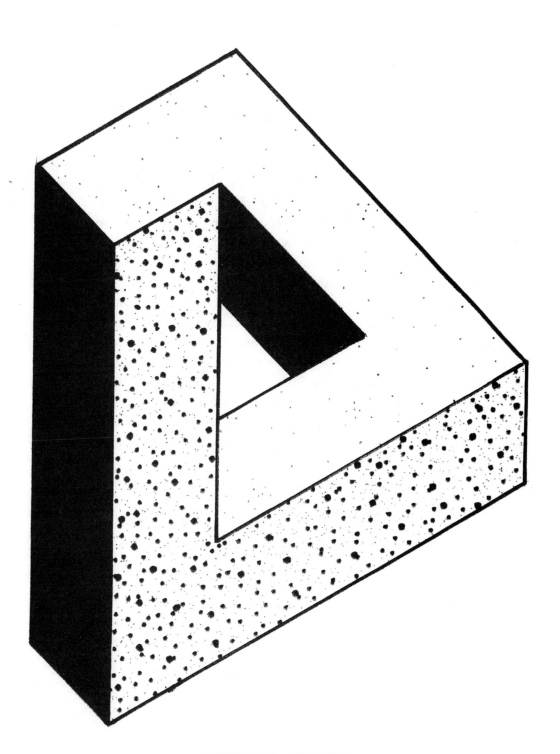

STUBBED TRIBAR

Celestial Quadra-Bar

FINALLY, we conclude this tour of Impossibilia with the "Celestial Quadra-Bar." This device is composed of single-entity elements, and you cannot tell for sure if they are joined or unjoined. Here, as in the "Space Fork," we experience a vibrant visual oscillation induced by the indecipherability of the figure. Even though impossible figures like this may be made up of the simplest of elements, they still retain the power to provide us with some most entertaining mental consternation.

With a single bar, which is not much to look at, you can't do much that is impossible except to reorient the ends in an impossible way, as in the "Opposing Timbers" on page 116. However, this well-integrated assembly of impossible bars shows what you can accomplish by connecting two or more of these single entities. When the simple bars are joined together in a "gang bar," as we see here, the overall figure takes on a whole new dimension. You might say that these very useful single-bar components are like the side limbs that someone swiped off the infamous "Impossible Triangle" and experimented with.

At your first encounter with the "Celestial Quadra-Bar" your eye-brain system automatically accepts the bars as solid objects. Then, when you start to see that they aren't really solid, you experience a struggle, since your mind's eye cannot decide what to do with them. The figure has a strong sense of solidity about it, especially at the top and bottom, but when you scan the opposing ends of the seemingly solid bars, they simply vanish into airy nothingness!

Now that you've read this book and have possibly already created a few impossible objects yourself, perhaps you may quit your present work as a person who deals in reality, and become an expert impossibler!

Have fun!

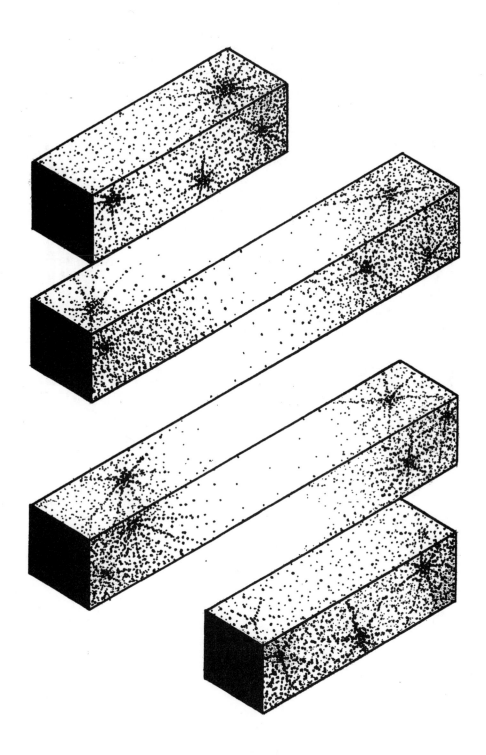

CELESTIAL QUADRA-BAR

"*. . . And he said, the things which are impossible with men are possible with God. For with God nothing shall be impossible.*"—Luke 18:27; 1:37

About the Author

The author, an architect and graphic artist, obtained his masters degree in Civil Engineering from Stanford University. He has since pursued a career in home planning and design. His interests include astronomy, geology, meteorology, photography, and optical illusions. He conducts lectures and seminars on astronomy, and his articles on this subject have appeared in several nationally known publications. He lives with his wife and three children near Sacramento, California.

Index

1-07 3 circ (06)